THE GAZE OF ORPHEUS

THE
GAZE
OF
ORPHEUS

and other literary essays

by

MAURICE
BLANCHOT

Preface by Geoffrey Hartman
Translated by Lydia Davis
Edited, with an Afterword,
by P. Adams Sitney

STATION HILL

The translation is based on the French editions copyright © 1943, 1949, 1955, 1959, 1969 by Editions Gallimard, as follows:
"De l'Angoisse au langage" from *Faux Pas* (1943); "Littérature et le droit à la mort" from *La Part du feu* (1949); "La Solitude essentielle," "Le Regard d'Orphée," "Lire," and "Les Deux Versions de l'imaginaire" from *L'Espace littéraire* (1955); "Le Chant des Sirènes" and "La Puissance et la gloire" from *Le Livre à venir* (1959); "Le Problème de Wittgenstein," "La Voix narrative," and "L'Absence du livre" from *L'Entretien infini* (1969).

Quotations from Hegel are from A.V. Miller's translation, *Phenomenology of Spirit* (Oxford: Oxford University Press, 1977).

Special thanks for assistance are due to Robert Lamberton (Translation Text Editor), Paul Auster (Consulting Editor), Michael Coffey (Proofreader), and Georges Borchardt, Inc. (Literary Agent).

Produced by Open Studio, Ltd., a non-profit production facility for writers, artists, and independent publishers, supported in part by grants from the National Endowment for the Arts and the New York State Council on the Arts.

The translation was made with assistance under the Comprehensive Employment and Training Act of the Department of Labor through a grant to Open Studio, Ltd. and Station Hill Press (Director/Publisher: George Quasha).

Published by Station Hill Press, Barrytown, New York 12507, with partial support from the National Endowment for the Arts and the New York State Council on the Arts.

Library of Congress Cataloging in Publication Data

Blanchot, Maurice, 1907—
    The gaze of Orpheus, & other literary essays.

    1. Literature—Addresses, essays, lectures.   I. Title.
PN45.B425   809   80-27297
ISBN 0-930794-37-0
ISBN 0-930794-38-9 (pbk.)

Manufactured in the United States of America

Other Books by Maurice Blanchot

In French:

Thomas l'obscur
Aminadab
Faux Pas
L'Arrêt de mort
Le Très-Haut
La Part du feu
Lautréamont et Sade
Thomas l'obscur (nouvelle version)
Au Moment voulu
Le Ressassement éternel
Celui qui ne m'accompagnait pas
L'Espace littéraire
Le Dernier Homme
Le Livre à venir
L'Attente l'oubli
L'Entretien infini
L'Amitié
La Folie du jour
Le Pas au-delà
L'Ecriture du désastre

In English:

Thomas the Obscure, *translated by Robert Lamberton*
Death Sentence, *translated by Lydia Davis*
The Madness of the Day (bi-lingual edition), *translated by Lydia Davis*

Contents

Preface
by Geoffrey Hartman

This selection from the critical writings of Maurice Blanchot can only be suggestive of a distinguished *oeuvre* that began in the 1930s and spans forty years. Yet the selection is exemplary for its clearly translated and well-chosen excerpts from Blanchot's many influential books. Reading him now, and in this form, I feel once more the excitement of discovering Blanchot in the 1950s; and I wonder why it took so long to introduce him to an English-speaking public. There are difficulties, of course: certain of his themes are obsessively elaborated and his text-milieu may appear exotic. His reading has absorbed vast amounts of Continental philosophy, including Hegel and Heidegger, and near-untranslatable poets such as Hölderlin and Mallarmé. But the difficulties his work presents pale before the intrinsic interest of his meditations. The time has come when his sort of mind—and prose—can be appreciated.

In the 1950s one was astonished at so intense a concentration on the "world" of the writer, as if the latter had his own element to live or die in, whatever the era, whatever the national language. Blanchot never removed his subjects from the writing-condition: from table, paper, ink, the act of naming or nouning, the fluent ease or the dread impersonality and anguish of writing as it performed Hegel's "labor of the Negative." Blanchot's critique of views of the incarnationist image or his stress on the complexity of fictional visualization made Anglo-American theories of organic form seem like a pastoral pursuit. According to Blanchot, writing is a fearful spiritual weapon that negates the naive existence of what it names and must therefore do the same to itself. Literature runs the danger of denying its own desire for presence, although it cannot (as Hegel thought) become anything else—philosophy, for example. Hence writing is a self-disturbed activity: it knows itself to be, at once, trivial and apocalyptic, vain yet of the greatest consciousness-altering potential. As Blanchot says, in the early amazing essay that opens this collection: "It seems comical and miserable that in order to manifest itself, dread, which opens and closes the sky, needs the activity of a man sitting at his table and forming letters on a piece of paper."

It would be wrong, however, to view Blanchot as a philosopher with mystical leanings, who has somehow wandered into the realm of art and cannot get out. From the beginning he was a journalist rather than a mystic, conceiving writing as an absolutely daily act, like politics. His earliest book of essays was gathered from embattled journals of his day. And the later criticism is best seen as a continuous, open-ended conversation or "infinite interview" with Romantic and post-Romantic authors. More precisely, with authors—literary, philosophical, theological—who have absorbed the shock of revolution (especially the French Revolution) and its Reign of Terror. That terror never ceases, according to Blanchot: it continues to shape the literature of our time. But the historical events also make writers aware of a revolutionary activity already within them: of a radically negative power, that of language.

After upheavals like the French Revolution, and again after the Holocaust, the dial of interest shifts from *significance* to *force*, and continues to quiver between them. There are those who say that writing makes no difference, that reflection cannot change the world; and there are those who insist that only thinkers who have experienced writing, or speech-acts equivalent to it—like parables in the New Testament or the negative utterances of Christ (*Noli me tangere*, "don't touch me")— know themselves enough to be a force for change. This understanding of language as the act of great poets or prosaists—and not as an abstract quiddity—is brought by Blanchot into studies of Kafka and Kierkegaard, of Flaubert and Wittgenstein, of Hölderlin, Hegel, Nietzsche and Rilke, of Melville and Mann, of Mallarmé, Roussel and Duras.

For what do I prize him most? His essays are living proof that literary criticism has its own reason for being. It is not the servant or fashionable expositor of the latest thought-system. We all know that in England and America criticism enjoys a doubtful status. As a philosopher you are something, even if you write on Nothing. But as a literary essayist you remain a no-thing, a hybrid or borderer between philosophy and literature, indecisive, or making indecisiveness your specialty. Blanchot, despite his emphasis on absence, death, and the nonaffirmative character of words, establishes the critic within this curious void—a form of life that, as Hegel said, "supports death and maintains itself within it."

Blanchot thinks texts through like a philosopher yet also thinks through texts; that is, he does not throw them away, having thought to understand them. Though he arrives in America after Sartre, Barthes, Foucault and Derrida, he is more literary than they are, and also more crucial to our sense of what a philosophical (not merely philosophy-inspired) criticism can be. His voice, at once loquacious and laconic, eloquent and elliptical, is far from comforting, because instead of story or narrative it evokes the parabolic and indirect, or interminable and interruptive, character of literary speech. It is itself full of dark insights, memorable formulations and Pascalian maxims.

I end with an extravagant claim. When we come to write the history of criticism for the 1940 to 1980 period, it will be found that Blanchot, together with Sartre, made French "discourse" possible, both in its relentlessness and its acuity. That "discourse", like many French things, is not to everyone's taste, yet it could prove more powerful and persistent than the notion of taste itself.

New Haven, CT
October 1980   Geoffrey H. Hartman

A Note on the Translation
by Lydia Davis

The challenge of translating Blanchot's work follows inevitably from the brilliance and complexity of his thought and style: the translator, a lonely sort of acrobat, becomes confused in a labyrinth of paradox, or climbs a pyramid of dependent clauses and has to invent a way down from it in his own language. The challenge, though, is not only to the translator, but also to the text: now it undergoes the closest of examinations, and every word is ferreted for its meaning. In some sense the text and the translator are locked in struggle—"I attacked that sentence, it resisted me, I attacked another, it eluded me"—a struggle in which, curiously, when the translator wins, the text wins too, and when the translator loses, what wins is the demon inhabiting the space between languages, champion of the inviolability of each language. And the demon says, in Blanchot's words, "The translator is guilty of a greater impiety. Enemy of God, he intends to rebuild the Tower of Babel."

The translator: "He lives on nothing but alms" (Valery Larbaud). Peculiar outcast, ghost in the world of literature, recreating in another form something already created, creating and not creating, writing words that are his own and not his own, writing a work not original to him, composing with utmost pains and without recognition of his pains or the fact that the composition really is his own. "A writer of singular originality precisely where he seems to have no claim to any. He is the secret master of the difference between languages . . . " (Blanchot). And courageous, for he must have the courage to destroy if he is to create.

The act of translation: the "idea" takes off in wild flight, and the translator pursues it every way he can, though even once it is caught, it may slip away again as he tries to bend it into another language: the soul of the text crossing from one body to another, expelled by a sneeze for one dangerous moment . . . Often what is contained between the first capital letter of a sentence and the final period is a complex problem, an entire project. Then the period comes to represent for the translator a moment during which he cannot be assaulted. He enters the next sentence, and he is entering another hazardous territory.

The translated work: curiously unlocated, an odd non-being. This is not an American work, and not a French work, but a version in English of a French work. The language here approximating another language, the words here in some sense pieced together—since *these* words and this thought were not born together, since these words have been imposed on this thought. And there are problems special to Blanchot's thought, among them: *récit* ("narrative," "account") as Blanchot uses it has a meaning deliberately distinct from that of *histoire* ("story," "narrative")—perhaps in its greater emphasis on the telling, the recital of events true or false— and here that distinction is preserved in the differentiation between "tale" and "story"; and Blanchot's *neutre* could be, almost equally, "neuter" or "neutral"—but "neuter" is closer to what seems to be a specifically grammatical reference.

And part of the idea is lost when it loses its own words: a word such as *manque* in French—both "lack" and "defect"— becomes in English either "lack" or "defect". The word *ouverture*—"opening" and "overture"—becomes one or the other. *Etre* is both "being" and "to be," as *écrire* is "to write" and "the act of writing" in general, though *écriture*, too, is "writing": "the act of writing" and "the thing written." The same problem in the opposite direction: a word like "work," which must stand in for both *oeuvre*, "work of art or literature," and *travail*, "labor."

When the French was particularly rich in meaning, the English had to be poorer, though often the correspondence was direct enough so that perhaps little was lost. Beyond the problems common to all translations of layered and much-meditated works, however, Blanchot's work contains its own extraordinary ambiguities—some that have baffled everyone called in to help, though reasonable solutions were eventually found. Among the meticulously critical readers of the book in manuscript were P. Adams Sitney, its Editor, who took it to heart as much as the translator did, and Michael Coffey, who voluntarily dedicated his time and skill as copyeditor to giving the book its finishing touches. Paul

Auster deserves special thanks for his constant encouragement and thoughtful advice, and for first pointing the way to the works of Maurice Blanchot. Finally, warmest appreciation goes to Robert Lamberton, himself an experienced translator of Blanchot, for the hard and patient work he did on the manuscript. Checking each essay sentence by sentence against the French, he questioned everything he found unclear or believed to be wrong, suggested alternatives which were most often adopted, caught several omissions of a phrase or a whole sentence, and occasionally rewrote an extremely difficult and complex sentence so that it came closer to the coherence of the original. He was the book's essential critic.

Lydia Davis
February, 1981

The Gaze of Orpheus

From Dread to Language

A writer who writes, "I am alone" or, like Rimbaud, "I am really from beyond the grave," can be considered rather comical. It is comical for a man to recognize his solitude by addressing a reader and by using methods that prevent the individual from being alone. The word *alone* is just as general as the word *bread*. To pronounce it is to summon to oneself the presence of everything the word excludes. These aporias in the language are rarely taken seriously. It is enough that the words do their duty and that literature does not cease to appear possible. The writer's "I am alone" has a simple meaning (no one near me) that the use of language contradicts in appearance only.

If we dwell on these difficulties, we risk discovering this: that the writer is under suspicion of a half lie. To Pascal, who complains of being abandoned in the world, Paul Valéry says, "A distress that writes well is not so complete that it hasn't salvaged from the shipwreck . . . "; but a distress that writes in a mediocre way deserves the same reproach. How can a person be alone if he confides to us that he is alone? He summons us in order to drive us away; he muses on us in order to persuade us that he is not musing on us; he speaks the language of men at the moment when there is no longer, for him, either language or man. It is easy to believe that this person, who ought to be separated from himself by despair, not only retains the thought of some other person but uses this solitude to create an effect that obliterates his solitude.

Is the writer only half sincere? That is really of little importance and it is clear that the reproach is a superficial one. Perhaps Pascal is so unhappy for the very reason that he writes brilliantly. The capacity that he retains of making himself admirable by expressing his misery enters into the horror of his condition as its most painful cause. Some people suffer because they cannot express completely what they feel. They are distressed by the obscurity of their feelings. They think they would be relieved if they could turn the confusion in which they are lost into precise words. But another suffers from being the fortunate interpreter of his misfortune. He suffocates in that intellectual freedom he still has and that allows him to see where he is. He is torn apart by the harmony of his images, by the air of happiness radiating from what he writes. He experiences this contradiction as the unavoidably oppressive aspect of the exaltation that he finds in that writing, an exaltation that crowns his disgust.

The writer could, of course, not write. That is true. Why would man at the farthest reach of solitude write, "I am alone," or, like Kierkegaard, "I am all alone here"? Who forces him into this activity, in a situation where, knowing nothing of himself or of anything else but a crushing absence, he becomes completely passive? Fallen into terror and despair, perhaps he will pace around and around like a hunted animal in a room. One can imagine that he lives deprived of the thought that would make him reflect his unhappiness, of the eyes that would let him perceive the face of that unhappiness, of the voice that would permit him to complain of it. Mad, wildly insane, he lacks the organs he needs to live with others and himself. But these images, however natural they may be, are not convincing. It is to the intelligent witness that the mute animal appears to be a victim of solitude. The person who is alone is not the one who experiences the impression of being alone; this monster of desolation needs the presence of another if his desolation is to have a meaning, another who, with his reason intact and his senses preserved, renders momentarily possible the distress that had until then been impotent.

A writer is not free to be alone without expressing the fact that he is alone. Even if he has reached the point where everything touching the act of writing has become vanity, he is still tied to arrangements of words; in fact, it is in the use of expression that he coincides most completely with the nothingness without expression that he has become. Precisely that which causes language to be destroyed in him also obliges him to use language. He is like a hemiplegic for whom the same illness constitutes both an obligation to walk and a prohibition against walking. He is forced to run ceaselessly in order to prove with each movement that he is deprived of movement. He is all the more paralyzed because of the fact that his limbs obey him. He suffers from the horror that turns his sound legs, his vigorous muscles, and the satisfying exercise he derives from them into the proof and the cause of the impossibility of his progress. In the same way that the distress of any man presupposes at a certain point that to be reasonable would be insane (he would like to lose his reason, but he discovers it in the very loss into which it is sinking), a person who writes is committed to writing by the silence and the privation of language that have stricken him. As long as he is not alone, he either writes or does not write; the hours he passes searching for and weighing words he senses only as something necessary to his calling, his pleasure, or his inspiration; he is deceiving himself when he speaks of an irresistible necessity. But if he lands at the outer limit of solitude, where the external considerations of art, knowledge, and the public disappear, he no longer has the freedom to be anything other than what his situation and the infinite disgust he feels would want absolutely to prevent him from being.

The writer finds himself in this more and more comical condition—of having nothing to write, of having no means of writing it, and of being forced by an extreme necessity to keep writing it. Having nothing to express should be taken in the simplest sense. Whatever he wants to say, it is nothing. The world, things, knowledge, are for him only reference points across the void. And he himself is already reduced to nothing. Nothing is his material. He rejects the forms in which it offers itself to him as being something. He wants to grasp it not in an allusion but in its own truth. He seeks it as the no that is not no to this, to that, to everything, but the pure and simple no. What is more, he does not seek it; it stands apart from all investigation; it cannot be taken as an end; one cannot propose to the will that it adopt as its end something that takes possession of the will by annihilating it: it is not, that is all there is to it; the writer's "I have nothing to say," like that of the accused, contains the whole secret of his solitary condition.

What makes these reflections difficult to pursue is that the word *writer* seems to designate an occupation rather than a human condition. A cobbler in a state of dread could laugh at himself for providing others with the means of walking while he himself is caught in a paralyzing trap. However, it does not occur to anyone to describe his dread as though it were characteristic of a man who repairs shoes. The feeling that produces dread is only accidentally linked to an object, and it reveals precisely that this object—on account of which one is losing oneself in an endless death—is insignificant to the feeling it provokes and to the man it is torturing. One dies at the thought that any object to which one is attached is lost, and in this mortal fear one also feels that this object is nothing, an interchangeable sign, an empty occasion. There is nothing that cannot feed dread, and dread is, more than anything else, this indifference to what creates it, although at the same time it seems to rivet the man to the cause it has chosen.

It sometimes seems, in a strange way, as though dread characterized the writer's function, and, stranger still, as though the fact of writing deepened the dread to the point of attaching it to him rather than to any other sort of man. There comes a moment when the literary man who writes out of loyalty to words writes out of loyalty to dread; he is a writer because this fundamental anxiety has revealed itself to him, and at the same time it reveals itself to him inasmuch as he is a writer; more than that, it seems to exist in the world only because there are, in the world, men who have pushed the art of signs to the point of language, and concern for language to the point of writing, which demands a particular will, a thoughtful consciousness, the protection and retention of the use of the powers of discourse. It is because of this that the case of the writer has something exorbitant and inadmissible about it. It seems comical and miserable that in order to manifest itself, dread, which opens and closes the sky, needs the activity of a man sitting at his table and forming letters on a piece of paper. This may well be shocking, but in the same way that the necessary condition for the solitude of a madman is the presence of a lucid witness. The existence of the writer is proof that within one individual there exist side by side both a man full of dread and one who is cool and calculating, both a madman and a reasonable being, a mute who has lost all words firmly wedded to an orator, master of discourse. The case of the writer is special because he represents the paradox of dread in a special way. Dread challenges all the realities of reason, its methods, its possibilities, its very capacity to exist, its ends, and yet dread forces reason to be there; it summons it to be reason as perfectly as it can; dread itself is only possible because there continues to exist in all its power the faculty that dread renders impossible, that it annihilates.

The sign of his importance is that the writer has nothing to say. This is laughable, too. But this joke has obscure requirements. First of all, it is not so usual for a man to have nothing to say. It may happen that a certain individual temporarily silences all the words that express him, by dismissing discursive knowledge, by seizing a current of silence that emerges from his deep inner life. Then, he says nothing, because the faculty of saying has been broken off; he is in an order where words are no longer in their places, have never existed, do not even propose themselves as a slight erasure of silence; he is entirely absent from what is being said. But for the writer the situation is different. He remains attached to discourse; he departs from reason only in order to be faithful to it; he has authority over language, and he can never completely send it away. Having nothing to say is for him characteristic of someone who always has something to say. In the center of garrulousness he finds the zone of laconicism where he must now remain.

This situation is full of torments and it is ambiguous. It cannot be confused with the sterility that sometimes overwhelms an artist. In fact, it is so different from this sterility that all the noble and rare thoughts he has, the abundance and success of the images, the flow of literary beauty, are what put the writer in a position to attain the emptiness that will be, in his art, the answer to the dread that fills his life. Not only has he not broken with words, but they come to him grander, more brilliant, more successful than they have ever been for him before; he is capable of the most varied works; there is a natural connection between his most exact thoughts and his most seductive writings; it is marvelously easy for him to join number and logic; his whole mind is language. This is the first sign that if he has nothing to say, it is not for lack of means, but because everything he can say is controlled by the nothingness that dread makes appear to him as his own object among the temporary objects that dread gives itself. It is towards this nothingness that all literary powers flow back, as towards the spring that must exhaust them, and this nothingness absorbs them not in an effort to be expressed by them, but rather to consume them with neither aim nor result. This is a singular phenomenon. The writer is called upon by his dread to perform a genuine sacrifice of himself. He must spend, he must consume, the forces that make him a writer. This spending must also be genuine.

Either to be content with not writing anymore, or to write a work in which all the values that the mind held in potential reappear in the form of effects, is to prevent the sacrifice from being made or to replace it by an exchange. What is required of the writer is infinitely more difficult. He must be destroyed, in an act that really puts him at stake. The exercise of his power forces him to sacrifice that power. The work he makes signifies that there is no work made. The art he uses is an art in which perfect success and complete failure must appear at the same time, the fullness of means and irremediable debasement, the reality and the nothingness of the results.

When someone composes a work, that work can be destined to serve a certain end—moral, religious, political—that is exterior to it; we say then that art is serving alien values; it is being exchanged in a practical way for certain realities, whose price it raises. But if the book is not useful for anything, it appears as a disruptive phenomenon in the totality of human relations, which are based on the equivalence of the currencies exchanged, on the principle that corresponding to every production of energy there should be a potential energy in a produced object, an energy capable of being thrown back again, in one form or another, into the uninterrupted circuit of forces; the book that art has produced and that cannot produce any other kind of value than that which it represents seems to be an exception to the law that is assumed in the maintainance of all existence; it expresses a disinterested effort; it profits, in a privileged or scandalous way, from an invaluable position; it is reduced to itself; it is art for art's sake. Nevertheless—and the endless discussions about art for art's sake show this— the work of art only appears, to insensitive eyes, to be an exception to the general law of exchanges. It is not useful for anything?—say the critics; but it is useful for something precisely because it is not useful for anything; its usefulness is to express that useless part without which civilization is not possible; or it is useful to art, which is one of man's goals or is a goal in itself or is the image of the absolute, etc . . . . We could elaborate on this subject in a thousand ways. This is all futile because it is clear that the work of art does not represent a true phenomenon of spending. On the contrary, it signifies an advantageous operation of transformation of energy. The author has produced more than himself; he has carried what he has received to a higher point of efficacy; he has been creative; and what he has created is from now on a source of values whose fecundity goes far beyond the forces spent to bring it into being.

The writer plunged into dread is himself painfully aware that art is not a ruinous operation; he is trying to lose himself (and to lose himself as a writer), and yet sees that by writing he increases the credit of humanity, and thus his own, since he is still a man; he gives art new hopes and riches that return to weigh him down; he transforms into forces of consolation the hopeless orders he receives; he saves with nothingness. This contradiction is so enormous that it seems to him no stratagem can put an end to it. The artist's traditional misfortunes—to live poor and miserable, to die as he completes his work—naturally do not figure in the structure of his future. The hope of the nihilist—to write a work, but a destructive work, representing, because of what it is, an undefined possiblity of things that will no longer be—is equally foreign to him. He sees into the intention of the first—who believes he is sacrificing his existence, whereas he is actually putting the whole of it into the work that is to eternalize it—and the naive scheme of the second, who offers men, in the form of limited upheavals, an infinite vision of renewal. His own path is different. He obeys dread, and dread orders him to lose himself, without that loss being compensated by any positive value.

"I do not want to attain something," the writer says to himself. "On the contrary, I want to prevent that something that I am when I write from resulting, because of the fact that I write, in anything, in any form. It is indispensable to me to be a writer who is infinitely smaller in his work than in himself, and this through the complete and honest use of all his means. I want this possiblity of creating, as it becomes creation, not only to express its own destruction along with the destruction of everything it challenges—that is to say everything—but also not to express it. For me it is a question of making a work that does not even have the reality of expressing the absence of reality. What retains the power of expression retains the greatest real value, even if what is expressed has none; but to be inexpressive does not put an end to the ambiguity which still derives from inexpressiveness the result that what is then expressed is the need to express nothing."

This monologue is fictitious, because the writer cannot set for himself as a project, in the form of a considered and coherent plan, that which he is required to hold as the very opposite of a project, with the most obscure and emptiest of constraints. Or, more precisely, his dread is increased by the exigency that forces him to pursue within a methodical task the concern which he cannot realize except through an act of immediate disruption of himself. His will, as the practical power to order what is possible, itself becomes full of dread. His clear reason, still capable of establishing a dialogue with itself, becomes, because it is clear and discursive, the equal of the impenetrable madness that reduces him to silence. Logic identifies with the unhappiness and fright of consciousness. However, this substitution can only be temporary. If the rule is to obey dread and if dread accepts only what increases it, for the time being it is tolerable to try to shift it to the level of a limited plan, because that effort carries it to a higher point of uneasiness, but this cannot last; active reason quickly imposes the stability that is its law; full of dread a moment before, now it turns dread into a reason; it turns anxious seeking into a chance for forgetfulness and repose. Once this usurpation has taken place, and even before it happens, just in the threat of it that is glimpsed even in the most carefully distrustful use of the creative mind, all work becomes impossible. Dread requires the abandonment of what threatens to make it weaker; it requires it, and this abandonment, by signifying the failure of the agreement that had been desired for its very difficulty, increases dread enormously; it even becomes so great that, freed of its means and losing contact with the contradictions in which it is sinking, it moves toward a strange satisfaction; as it reduces itself, it no longer sees more than itself, it is contemplation that veils itself and perception that fragments itself; a sort of sufficiency comes into being along with its insufficiency; the devastating movement that it is draws it toward a definitive splitting apart; it will lose itself in the current that is inducing it to lose everything. But at this new extremity, the kind of dread dissolving into drunkenness that it feels itself becoming impels it towards the outside again. With increased heaviness, dread comes back to the logical expression that makes it feel—in a reasonable way, that is, a way deprived of delights—the contradictions that keep putting it back in the present. Creation is attempted again, all the more somber because it is attempted more violently and all the more meticulous because the memory of failure points to the fact that it is threatened by a new failure. Work is temporarily possible in the impossibility that weighs it down. And this continues to be the case until that very possibility presents itself as real, by destroying the share of impossibility that was its condition.

The writer cannot do without his project, since the depth of his dread is tied to the fact that this dread cannot do without methodic realization. But he is tempted by bizarre projects. For example, he wants to write a book in which the operation of all his forces of meaning will be reabsorbed into the meaningless. (Is the meaningless that which escapes objective intelligibility? These pages composed of a discontinuous series of words, these words that do not presume any language, can always, in the absence of an assignable meaning, and through the harmony or discordance of sounds, produce an effect that represents their justification.) Or else he proposes to himself a work from which the possibility of a reader will be excluded. (Lautréamont seems to have had this dream. How not to be read? One would like to arrange the book to resemble a house that would open easily to visitors; yet as soon as they went into it, they would not only have to get lost there, they would be caught in a treacherous trap; once there they would cease to be what they had been, they would die. What if the writer destroyed his work as soon as he had written it? That happens; it is a childish subterfuge; nothing has been accomplished so long as the structure of the work does not make the reader impossible, that reader being first of all the writer himself. One can imagine a book to which the author, man on the one hand, insect on the other, could have access only in the act of writing it; a book that would destroy him as capacity to read, without abolishing him as reason writing; that would take away from him the sight, the memory, the understanding of what he had composed with all his strength and all his mind.) Or again, he contemplates a work so foreign to his dread that it is its echo, because of the silence it keeps. (But the incognito is never real; any banal sentence attests to the despair that exists in the depths of language.)

It is because of the puerile nature of all these artifices that they are pondered and formulated with such gravity. Childishness anticipates its failure by taking upon itself a mode of being too slight for it to be

sanctioned by success or lack of success. These attempts have in common the fact that they are seeking a complete solution to a situation that
would be ruined and transformed into its opposite by a complete solution. These attempts do not have to fail, but they must not succeed.
Neither do they have to balance success and failure in a deliberate
pattern, so that ambiguity is left with the responsibility for the decision.
All the projects we have mentioned can in fact be reduced to ambiguity
and are not even conceivable outside the protection of a multifaceted
intention. The writer can get this loss of meaning—the meaning which
he requires of a text deprived of all intelligibility—from the most reasonable of texts if the latter seems to advertise its obviousness as a challenge
to immediate comprehension. To this he adds the further obscurity,
that there is doubt about the nonsense of this sense, that as reason plays
its customary tricks on itself, it only dies in the game because it
obstinately refuses to play. The ambiguity is such that one cannot take it
at its word either as reason or as unreason. Perhaps the page that is
absurd because it is sensible really is sensible; perhaps it does not make
the slightest sense; how does one decide? Its nature is linked to a change
in perspective, and there is nothing in it that allows it to be fixed in a
definitive light. (One can always say that its meaning is to admit of both
interpretations, to disguise itself sometimes as good sense, sometimes as
nonsense, and thereby to be determined as indetermination between
these two possibilities; but that in itself betrays the structure of the page,
because it is not postulated that the truth of the page is to be sometimes
one thing and sometimes another; on the contrary, it is possible that it is
uniquely this, uniquely that; it imperiously demands this choice; to the
indetermination in which we try to grasp it, it adds the claim that it is
also absolutely determined by one or the other of the two terms between
which it oscillates.)

Yet ambiguity is not a solution for the writer who is full of dread. It
cannot be conceived as a solution. As soon as it is part of a project and
appears as the expression of a scheme, it gives up the multiplicity which
is its nature, and freezes in the form of an artifice whose exterior complexity is constantly being reduced by the intention that has brought it
into being. I can read a poem with a double, triple, or perhaps no
meaning, but I do not hesitate over the meaning of these varied mean-

ings and in this I see a determination to reach myself through the enigma. Where the enigma shows itself as such, it vanishes. It is only an enigma when it does not exist in itself, when it hides itself so deeply that it slips away into what causes its nature to be to slip away. The writer who is full of dread encounters his dread as an enigma, but he cannot have recourse to the enigma in order to obey the dread. He cannot believe that by writing under a mask, by borrowing pseudonyms, by making himself unknown, he is putting himself right with the solitude which he is fated to apprehend in the very act of writing. Since he is an enigma himself, an enigma as writer who must write and not write, it is not within his means to use enigma in order to be faithful to his enigmatic nature. He knows himself as torment, but this torment is not enclosed in a particular feeling, it is no more sadness than it is joy, nor is it knowledge experienced in the unknowable that underlies it: it is a torment that uses everything to justify itself and gets rid of everything, that espouses any object at all and escapes, through every object, the absence of object; that appears to be apprehensible in the shiver which binds death to the feeling of being, but that makes death ridiculous in the sight of the void it hollows out; that nevertheless does not allow one to send it away, that on the contrary demands that one submit to it and desire it, and makes deliverance from it into a worse torment, burdened by what makes it lighter. To say of this torment: I obey it by abandoning my written thought to oscillation, by expressing it through a code, would be to represent it as interesting me only in the mystery in which it reveals itself; however, I no more know it as mysterious than as familiar, neither as a key to a world which has no key, nor as an answer to the absence of a question; if it consigns me to enigma, it does so by refusing to link me to enigma; if it tears me apart with obviousness, it does so precisely by tearing me apart; it is there—of that I am certain—but it is there in the dark, and I cannot maintain that certainty except in the collapse of all the conditions of certainty, and first of all in the collapse of what I am when I am certain it is there.

If ambiguity were the essential mode of revelation for the man full of dread, we would have to believe that dread has something to reveal to him that he nevertheless cannot grasp, that it puts him in the presence of an object whose dizzying absence is all that he feels, that it conveys to

him, through failure and also through the fact that failure does not put
an end to anything, a supreme possibility which he must, as a man,
renounce, but whose meaning and truth he can at least understand in
the existence of dread. Ambiguity presupposes a secret that no doubt
expresses itself by vanishing, but that in this vanishing allows itself to be
glimpsed as a possible truth. There is a beyond in which, if I reached it, I
would perhaps be reaching only myself, but which also has a meaning
outside me, and even for me has no other meaning than that of being
absolutely outside me. Ambiguity is the language used by a messenger
who tries to teach me what I cannot learn and who completes his
instruction by warning me that I am learning nothing of what he is
teaching me. Such an equivocal belief is not absent from certain moments of dread. But the dread itself can only tear it apart in every positive
aspect it still retains. Dread transforms it into a weight that is crushing
and that nevertheless amounts to nothing at all. It changes this speaking
mouth, this mouth that speaks ably through the confusion of tongues,
through silence, through truth, through falsehood, into an organ condemned to speak passionately in order to say nothing. It retains
ambiguity, but it takes its task away from it. All that it allows to survive,
of this misreading which keeps the mind in suspense through the hope
of an unknowable truth, is the labyrinth of multiple meanings in which
the mind continues its search without any hope of a possible truth.

Dread has nothing to reveal and is itself indifferent to its own revelation. It is not concerned about whether or not anyone reveals it; it draws
anyone who has tied himself to it towards a mode of being in which the
need to make oneself the subject of one's speech is already obsolete.
Kierkegaard made of the demoniac one of the most profound forms of
dread and the demoniac refuses to communicate with the outside, it
does not want to make itself manifest; if it wanted to, it would not be able
to; it is confined within that which makes it inexpressible; it is filled with
dread by solitude and by the fear that this solitude might be broken. But
the point is that for Kierkegaard, the mind must reveal itself, dread
comes from the fact that, all direct communication being impossible,
the only authentic way to go towards the other seems to be to enclose
oneself in the most isolated interiority, and this path itself is a dead end
unless it insists on being recognized as a dead end. However, even

though dread weighs like a stone on the individual, crushing and tearing to shreds what he has in common with men, it does not stop with this tragedy of mutilation, but turns on individuality itself, on the insane, tattered, harrowing aspiration to be only oneself, in order to force it out of its refuge, in which to live is to live sequestered. Dread does not allow the recluse to be alone. It deprives him of the means by which he could have some relation to another, making him more alien to his reality as a man than if he had suddenly been changed into some sort of vermin; but once he has been stripped in this way, and is about to bury himself in his monstrous particularity, dread throws him back out of himself and, in a new torment that he experiences as a suffocating irradiation, it confounds him with what he is not, turning his solitude into an expression of his communication and this communication into the meaning assumed by his solitude and drawing from this synonymy a new reason to be dread added to dread.

The writer does not write in order to express the concern that is his law. He writes without a goal, in an act that nevertheless has all the characteristics of a deliberate composition, and his concern for it craves realization at each instant. He is not trying to express his self full of dread any more than he is trying to express his self lost to itself; he has no use for this anxiety that wants to manifest itself as though by manifesting itself it dreamed it was saving itself; he is not its spokesman or the spokesman of some inaccessible truth within it; he is responding to a demand, and the response he makes public has nothing to do with that demand. Is there a vertigo in dread that prevents it from being communicated? In a sense yes, since it appears unfathomable; man cannot describe his torment, his torment escapes him; he believes that he will not be able to express what it is all about; he says to himself: I will never convey this suffering faithfully. But the point is that he imagines there is something to convey; he conceives his situation on the model of all other human situations; he wants to formulate its content; he pursues its meaning. In reality, dread has no mysterious underside; it exists completely in the obviousness that makes us feel it is there; it is entirely revealed as soon as one says: I am full of dread. One can write volumes to express what it is not, one can describe it in its most remarkable psychological forms, one can relate it to fundamental metaphysical notions;

there will be nothing more in all this rubbish than there is in the words *I am full of dread*, and these words themselves signify that there exists nothing else but dread.

Why should dread feel reluctant to be summoned outside? It is just as much the outside as the inside. The man to whom it has revealed itself (which does not mean that it has shown him the depths of its nature, since it has no depths), the man it has grasped in a profound way allows himself to be seen in the various expressions in which dread attracts him; he does not show himself complacently and he does not hide himself scrupulously; he is not jealous of his privacy, he neither flees nor seeks what shatters it; he cannot attach definitive importance to his solitude or to his union with another; full of dread when he withholds himself, full of dread even more when he gives himself, he feels he is bound to a necessity that cannot be altered by the yes or no of reality. Now it must be admitted that the writer who perceives the whole paradox of his task in the passion that is constantly hidden and that he constantly wants to lay bare, is realizing his torture, making a thing out of it, presenting it to himself as an object to be represented, one that is undoubtedly inaccessible, but nevertheless analogous to all the objects that it is the role of art to express. Why should the unhappiness of his condition be that he has to represent that condition—with the consequence that if he succeeds in representing it, his unhappiness will be changed into joy, his destiny fulfilled? He is not a writer because of his unhappiness, and his unhappiness does not come from the fact that he is a writer, but placed before the necessity of writing, he can no longer escape it, once he submits to it as an unrealizable task, unrealizable no matter what its form, and yet possible in that impossibility.

I have nothing to say about my dread, and it is not because it is seeking to be expressed that it stalks me as soon as I let myself fall silent. But dread also causes me to have nothing to say about anything, and it stalks me no less when I try to justify my task by giving it an end. However, I am not permitted to write just anything at all. The feeling that what I am doing is useless is connected to that other feeling, that nothing is more serious. It is not as the result of an order declaring to me: everything is permitted, do what you want, that I find myself before the expiration of the anything at all; it is as a limit to a situation that turns everything important to me into the equivalent of an anything at all and refuses me this anything at all precisely when it has become nothing to me. I can play my destiny in a game of dice, as long as I play it as chance exterior to me and accept it as a destiny absolutely tied to me; but if the dice are there in order to change into a whim the too burdensome fatality that I am no longer able to want, it is now in my interest to play and because of that interest in the game, I become a gambler who makes the game impossible (it is no longer a game). In the same way, if the writer wants to draw lots for what he writes, he can only do it if this operation represents the same necessity of reflection, the same search for language, the same cumbersome and useless effort as the act of writing. This is to say that for him, drawing lots is writing, writing while making both his mind and the use of his gifts the equivalent of pure chance.

It will always be harder for man to use his reason rigorously and adhere to it as to a coincidence of fortuitous events than to force it to imitate the effects of chance. It is relatively easy to elaborate a text with any letters at all taken at random. It is more difficult to compose that text while feeling the necessity of it. But it is extremely arduous to produce the most conscious and the most balanced sort of work while at each instant comparing the forces of reason that produce it to an actual game of caprice. It is in this sense that the rules defining the art of writing, the constraints placed upon it, the fixed forms that transform it into a necessary system—insurmountable obstacles to the throw of the dice—are all the more important for the writer because they make more exhausting the act of consciousness by which reason, following these very rules, must identify itself with an absence of rules. The writer who frees himself of precepts to rely on chance is failing to meet the requirement that commands him to experience chance only in the form of a mind subject to precepts. He tries to escape his creative intelligence, experienced as chance, by surrendering himself directly to chance. He appeals to the dice of the unconscious because he cannot play dice with extreme consciousness. He limits chance to chance. This is the basis of his quest for texts ravaged by randomness and his attempt to come to terms with negligence. It seems to him that by doing this he is closer to his nocturnal passion. But the point is that for him, the day is still there next to the night, and he needs to betray himself through fidelity to the norms of clarity, for the sake of what is without form and without law.

Acceptance of the rules has this limit: that when they have been obliterated and have become habits, they retain almost nothing of their form as constraints and have the spontaneity of that which is fortuitous. Most of the time, to give oneself to language is to abandon oneself. One allows oneself to be carried away by a mechanism that takes upon itself all the responsibility of the act of writing. True automatic writing is the habitual form of writing, writing that has used the mind's deliberate efforts and its erasures to create automatisms. The opposite of automatic writing is a dread-filled desire to transform the gifts of chance into deliberate initiatives, and, more specifically, the concern to take upon oneself, as a power in every way similar to chance, the consciousness that adheres to rules or invents them. The instinct that leads us, in dread, to flee from the rules—if it is not itself flight from dread—comes, then, from the need to pursue these rules as true rules, as an exacting kind of coherence, and no longer as the conventions and means of a traditional commodity. I try to give myself a new law, and I do not seek it because it is new or because it will be mine—this consideration of novelty or originality would be ridiculous in my position— but because its novelty is the guarantee that it is really a law, for me, a law that imposes itself with a rigor I am aware of and that impresses more heavily upon me the feeling that it has no more meaning than a toss of the dice.

Words give to the person who writes them the impression of being dictated to him by usage, and he receives them with the uneasy feeling of finding in them an immense reservoir of fluency and fully staged effects—staged without his power having had any part in it. This uneasiness can lead him to reject completely the words that belong to practical life, to break off the familiar voice he listens to so nonchalantly, less absorbed by what he writes under its influence than by the gestures and instructions of the croupier at the gaming table. It then seems to him necessary to resume responsibility for words, and, by sacrificing them in their servile capacity—precisely in their fitness to be of service to him— to recover, with their revolt, the power he has to be master of them. The object of the ideal of "words set free" is not to release words from all rules, but to free them from a rule one no longer submits to, in order to subject them to a law one really feels. There is an effort to make the act of writing the cause of a storm of order and a paroxysm of consciousness all the more filled with dread because this consciousness of a faultless organization is also the consciousness of an absolute failure of order. Regarded in this light, it quickly becomes clear that to invent new rules is no more legitimate than to reinvent the old rules; on the contrary, it is harder to give usage back its value as a constraint, to awaken in ordinary language the order that has been effaced from it, to adhere to habit as to the summons of reflection itself. To give a purer meaning to the words of the tribe can be to give words a new meaning, but it is also to give words their old meaning, to grant them the meaning they have, by reviving them as they have not ceased to be.

If I read, language, whether logical or completely musical (non-discursive), makes me adhere to a common meaning which, because it is not directly connected to what I am, interposes itself between my dread and me. But if I write, I am the one who is making the common meaning adhere to language, and in this act of signification I carry my forces, as much as I can, to their highest point of effectiveness, which is to give a meaning. Everything in my mind, therefore, strives to be a necessary connection and a tested value; everything in my memory strives to be the recollection of a language that has not yet been invented and the invention of a language that one recollects; to each operation there corresponds a meaning, and to these operations as a group, there corresponds that other meaning that there is no distinct meaning for each of them; words have their meaning as the substitute for an idea, but also as a composition of sounds and as a physical reality; images signify themselves as images, and thoughts affirm the twofold necessity that associates them with certain expressions and makes them thoughts of other thoughts. It is then that one can say that everything written has, for the one who writes it, the greatest meaning possible, but has also this meaning, that it is a meaning bound to chance, that it is nonmeaning. Naturally, since esthetic consciousness is only conscious of a part of what it does, the effort to attain absolute necessity and through it absolute futility is itself always futile. It cannot succeed, and it is this impossibility of succeeding, of reaching the end, where it would be as though it had never succeeded, that makes it constantly possible. It retains a little meaning from the fact that it never receives all its meaning, and it is filled with dread because it cannot be pure dread. The unknown masterpiece always allows one to see in the corner the tip of a charming foot, and this delicious foot prevents the work from being finished, but also prevents the painter from facing the emptiness of his canvas and saying, with the greatest feeling of repose: "Nothing, nothing! At last, there is nothing."

Literature
And the Right to Death

One can certainly write without asking why one writes. As a writer watches his pen form the letters, does he even have a right to lift it and say to it: "Stop! What do you know about yourself? Why are you moving forward? Why can't you see that your ink isn't making any marks, that although you may be moving ahead freely, you're moving through a void, that the reason you never encounter any obstacles is that you never left your starting place? And yet you write—you write on and on, disclosing to me what I dictate to you, revealing to me what I know; as others read, they enrich you with what they take from you and give you what you teach them. Now you have done what you did not do; what you did not write has been written: you are condemned to be indelible."

Let us suppose that literature begins at the moment when literature becomes a question. This question is not the same as a writer's doubts or scruples. If he happens to ask himself questions as he writes, that is his concern; if he is absorbed by what he is writing and indifferent to the possibility of writing it, if he is not even thinking about anything, that is his right and his good luck. But one thing is still true: as soon as the page has been written, the question which kept interrogating the writer while he was writing—though he may not have been aware of it—is now present on the page; and now the same question lies silent within the work, waiting for a reader to approach—any kind of reader, shallow or profound; this question is addressed to language, behind the person who is writing and the person who is reading, by language which has become literature.

This concern that literature has with itself may be condemned as an infatuation. It is useless for this concern to speak to literature about its nothingness, its lack of seriousness, its bad faith; this is the very abuse of which it is accused. Literature professes to be important while at the same time considering itself an object of doubt. It confirms itself as it disparages itself. It seeks itself: this is more than it has a right to do, because literature may be one of those things which deserve to be found but not to be sought.

Perhaps literature has no right to consider itself illegitimate. But the question it contains has properly speaking nothing to do with its value or its rights. The reason the meaning of this question is so difficult to discover is that the question tends to turn into a prosecution of art and art's capacities and goals. Literature is built on top of its own ruins: this paradox has become a cliché to us. But we must still ask whether the challenge brought against art by the most illustrious works of art in the last thirty years is not based on the redirection, the displacement, of a force laboring in the secrecy of works and loath to emerge into broad daylight, a force the thrust of which was originally quite distinct from any deprecation of literary activity or the literary Thing.

We should point out that as its own negation, literature has never signified the simple denunciation of art or the artist as mystification or deception. Yes, literature is unquestionably illegitimate, there is an underlying deceitfulness in it. But certain people have discovered something beyond this: literature is not only illegitimate, it is also null, and as long as this nullity is isolated in a state of purity it may constitute an extraordinary force, a marvellous force. To make literature become the exposure of this emptiness inside, to make it open up completely to its nothingness, realize its own unreality—this is one of the tasks undertaken by surrealism. Thus we are correct when we recognize surrealism as a powerful negative movement, but no less correct when we attribute to it the greatest creative ambition, because if literature coincides with nothing for just an instant, it is immediately everything, and this everything begins to exist: what a miracle!

It is not a question of abusing literature, but rather of trying to understand it and to see why we can only understand it by disparaging it. It has been noted with amazement that the question "What is literature?" has received only meaningless answers. But what is even stranger is that something about the very form of such a question takes away all its seriousness. People can and do ask "What is poetry?", "What is art?", and even "What is the novel?" But the literature which is both poem and novel seems to be the element of emptiness present in all these serious things, and to which reflection, with its own gravity, cannot direct itself without losing its seriousness. If reflection, imposing as it is, approaches literature, literature becomes a caustic force, capable of destroying the very capacity in itself and in reflection to be imposing. If reflection withdraws, then literature once again becomes something important, essential, more important than the philosophy, the religion or the life of the world which it embraces. But if reflection, shocked by this vast power, returns to this force and asks it what is it, it is immediately penetrated by a corrosive, volatile element and can only scorn a Thing so vain, so vague, and so impure, and in this scorn and this vanity be consumed in turn, as the story of Monsieur Teste has so clearly shown us.

It would be a mistake to say that the powerful negative contemporary movements are responsible for this volatizing and volatile force which literature seems to have become. About one hundred fifty years ago, a man who had the highest idea of art that anyone can have—because he saw how art can become religion and religion art—this man (called Hegel[1]) described all the ways in which someone who has chosen to be a man of letters condemns himself to belong to the "animal kingdom of the mind." From his very first step, Hegel virtually says, a person who wishes to write is stopped by a contradiction: in order to write, he must have the talent to write. But gifts, in themselves, are nothing. As long as he has not yet sat down at his table and written a work, the writer is not a writer and does not know if he has the capacity to become one. He has no talent until he has written, but he needs talent in order to write.

This difficulty illuminates, from the outset, the anomaly which is the essence of literary activity and which the writer both must and must not overcome. A writer is not an idealistic dreamer, he does not contemplate himself in the intimacy of his beautiful soul, he does not

---

[1] In this argument, Hegel is considering human work in general. It should be understood that the remarks which follow are quite remote from the text of the *Phenomenology* and make no attempt to illuminate it. The text can be read in Jean Hippolyte's translation and pursued further through his important book, *Genèse et structure de la Phénoménologie de l'esprit de Hegel*.

submerse himself in the inner certainty of his talents. He puts his talents to work; that is, he needs the work he produces in order to be conscious of his talents and of himself. The writer only finds himself, only realizes himself, through his work; before his work exists, not only does he not know who he is, but he is nothing. He only exists as a function of the work; but then how can the work exist? "An individual," says Hegel, "cannot know what he [really] is until he has made himself a reality through action. However, this seems to imply that he cannot determine the *End* of his action until he has carried it out; but at the same time, since he is a *conscious* individual, he must have the action in front of him beforehand as *entirely his* own, i.e. as an *End*."[2] Now, the same is true for each new work, because everything begins again from nothing. And the same is also true when he creates a work part by part: if he does not see his work before him as a project already completely formed, how can he make it the conscious end of his conscious acts? But if the work is already present in its entirety in his mind and if this presence is the essence of the work (taking the words for the time being to be inessential), why would he realize it any further? Either: as an interior project it is everything it ever will be, and from that moment the writer knows everything about it that he can learn, and so will leave it to lie there in its twilight, without translating it into words, without writing it—but then he won't ever write: and he won't be a writer. Or: realizing that the work cannot be planned, but only carried out, that it has value, truth and reality only through the words which unfold it in time and inscribe it in space, he will begin to write, but starting from nothing and with nothing in mind—like a nothingness working in nothingness, to borrow an expression of Hegel's.

In fact, this problem could never be overcome if the person writing expected its solution to give him the right to begin writing. "For that very reason," Hegel remarks, "he has to start immediately, and, whatever the circumstances, without further scruples about beginning, means, or End, proceed to action."[3] This way, he can break the circle, because in

---

[2] Hegel, *Phenomenology of Spirit*, trans. A.V. Miller, p. 240, Oxford University Press, 1977; Chapter V, Section 1a, "The spiritual animal kingdom and deceit or the 'matter in hand' itself."—*Tr.*

[3] *idem.* —*Tr.*

his eyes the circumstances under which he begins to write become the same thing as his talent, and the interest he takes in writing, and the movement which carries him forward, induce him to recognize these circumstances as his own, to see his own goal in them. Valéry often reminded us that his best works were created for a chance commission and were not born of personal necessity. But what did he find so remarkable about that? If he had set to work on *Eupalinos* of his own accord, what reasons would he have had for doing it? That he had held a piece of shell in his hand? Or that opening a dictionary one morning he happened to read the name Eupalinos in *La Grande Encyclopédie*? Or that he wanted to try dialogue as a form and happened to have on hand a piece of paper that lent itself to that form? One can imagine the most trivial circumstance as the starting point of a great work; nothing is compromised by that triviality: the act by which the author makes it into a crucial circumstance is enough to incorporate it into his genius and his work. In this sense, the publication *Architectures* which commissioned *Eupalinos* from Valéry was really the form in which he originally had the talent to write it: that commission was the beginning of that talent, was that talent itself, but we must also add that that commission only became real, only became a true project through Valéry's existence, his talent, his conversations in the world and the interest he had already shown in this sort of subject. Every work is an occasional work: this simply means that each work has a beginning, that it begins at a certain moment in time and that that moment in time is part of the work, since without it the work would have been only an insurmountable problem, nothing more than the impossibility of writing it.

Let us suppose that the work has been written: with it the writer is born. Before, there was no one to write it; starting from the book, an author exists and merges with his book. When Kafka chances to write the sentence, "He was looking out the window," he is—as he says—in a state of inspiration such that the sentence is already perfect. The point is that he is the author of it—or rather that because of it, he is an author: it is the source of his existence, he has made it and it makes him, it is himself and he is completely what it is. This is the reason for his joy, his pure and perfect joy. Whatever he might write, "the sentence is already perfect." This is the reason for his joy, his pure and perfect joy. This is the strange and profound certainty which art makes into a goal for itself.

What is written is neither well nor badly written, neither important nor frivolous, memorable nor forgettable: it is the perfect act through which what was nothing when it was inside emerges into the monumental reality of the outside as something which is necessarily true, as a translation which is necessarily faithful, since the person it translates exists only through it and in it. One could say that this certainty is in some sense the writer's inner paradise and that *automatic writing* has only been one way of making this golden age real—what Hegel calls the pure joy of passing from the night of possibility into the daytime of presence—or again, the certainty that what bursts into the light is none other than what was sleeping in the night. But what is the result of this? The writer who is completely gathered up and enclosed in the sentence "He was looking out the window" apparently cannot be asked to justify this sentence, since for him nothing else exists. But at least the sentence exists, and if it really exists to the point of making the person who wrote it a writer, this is because it is not just his sentence, but a sentence that belongs to other people, people who can read it—it is a universal sentence.

At this point, a disconcerting ordeal begins. The author sees other people taking an interest in his work, but the interest they take in it is different from the interest that made it a pure expression of himself, and that different interest changes the work, transforms it into something different, something in which he does not recognize the original perfection. For him the work has disappeared, it has become a work belonging to other people, a work which includes them and does not include him, a book which derives its value from other books, which is original if it does not resemble them, which is understood because it is a reflection of them. Now the writer cannot disregard this new stage. As we have seen, he exists only in his work, but the work exists only when it has become this public, alien reality, made and unmade by colliding with other realities. So he really is inside the work, but the work itself is disappearing. This is a particularly critical moment in the experiment. All sorts of interpretations come into play in getting beyond it. The writer, for example, would like to protect the perfection of the written Thing by keeping it as far away from life outside as possible. The work is what he created, not the book that is being bought, read, ground up and praised or demolished in the marketplace of the world. But then where does the work begin, where does it end? At what moment does it come into existence? Why make it public if the splendor of the pure self must be preserved in the work, why take it outside, why realize it in words which belong to everyone? Why not withdraw into an enclosed and secret intimacy without producing anything but an empty object and a dying echo? Another solution—the writer himself agrees to do away with himself: the only one who matters in the work is the person who reads it. The reader makes the work; as he reads it, he creates it; he is its real author, he is the consciousness and the living substance of the written thing; and so the author now has only one goal, to write for that reader and to merge with him. A hopeless endeavor. Because the reader has no use for a work written for him, what he wants is precisely an alien work in which he can discover something unknown, a different reality, a separate mind capable of transforming him and which he can transform into himself. An author who is writing specifically for a public is not really writing: it is the public that is writing, and for this reason the public can no longer be a reader; reading only appears to exist, actually it is nothing. This is why works created to be read are meaningless: no one reads them. This is why it is dangerous to write for other people, in order to evoke the speech of others and reveal them to themselves: the fact is that other people do not want to hear their own voices; they want to hear someone else's voice, a voice that is real, profound, troubling like the truth.

   A writer cannot withdraw into himself, for he would then have to give up writing. As he writes, he cannot sacrifice the pure night of his own possibilities, because his work is alive only if that night—and no other—becomes day, if what is most singular about him and farthest removed from existence as already revealed now reveals itself within shared existence. It is true that the writer can try to justify himself by setting himself the task of writing—the simple operation of writing, made conscious of itself quite independently of its results. As we know, this was Valéry's way of saving himself. Let us accept this. Let us accept that a writer may concern himself with art as pure technique, with technique as nothing more than the search for the means by which what was previously not written comes to be written. But if the experiment is to be a valid one, it cannot separate the operation from its results, and the results are never stable or definitive, but infinitely varied and meshed with a future which cannot be grasped. A writer who claims he is only concerned with how the work comes into being sees his concern get sucked into the world, lose itself in the whole of history; because the work is also made outside of him, and all the rigor he put into the consciousness of his deliberate actions, his careful rhetoric, is soon absorbed into the workings of a vital contingency which he cannot control or even observe. Yet his experiment is not worthless: in writing, he has put himself to the test as a nothingness at work, and after having written he puts his work to the test as something in the act of disappearing. The work disappears, but the fact of disappearing remains and appears as the essential thing, the movement which allows the work to be realized as it enters the stream of history, to be realized as it disappears. In this experiment, the writer's real goal is no longer the ephemeral work, but something beyond that work: the truth of the work, where the individual who writes—a force of creative negation—seems to join with the work in motion through which this force of negation and surpassing asserts itself.

This new notion, which Hegel calls the Thing Itself, plays a vital role in the literary undertaking. No matter that it has so many different meanings: it is the art which is above the work, the ideal that the work seeks to represent, the World as it is sketched out in the work, the values at stake in the creative effort, the authenticity of this effort; it is everything which, above the work that is constantly being dissolved in things, maintains the model, the essence and the spiritual truth of that work just as the writer's freedom wanted to manifest it and can recognize it as its own. The goal is not what the writer makes, but the truth of what he makes. As far as this goes, he deserves to be called an honest, disinterested conscience—*l'honnête homme*. But here we run into trouble: as soon as honesty comes into play in literature, imposture is already present. Here bad faith is truth, and the greater the pretention to morality and seriousness, the more surely will mystification and deceit triumph. Yes, literature is undoubtedly the world of values, since above the mediocrity of the finished works everything they lack keeps appearing as their own truth. But what is the result of this? A perpetual enticement, an extraordinary game of hide-and-seek in which the writer claims as an excuse that what he has in mind is not the ephemeral work but the spirit of that work and of every work—no matter what he does, no matter what he has not been able to do, he adapts himself to it, and his honest conscience derives knowledge and glory from it. Let us listen to that honest conscience; we are familiar with it because it is working in all of us. When the work has failed, this conscience is not troubled: it says to itself, "Now it has been fully completed, for failure is its essence; its disappearance constitutes its realization," and the conscience is happy with this; lack of success delights it. But what if the book does not even manage to be born, what if it remains a pure nothing? Well, this is still better: silence and nothingness are the essence of literature, "the Thing Itself." It is true: the writer is willing to put the highest value on the meaning his work has for him alone. Then it does not matter whether the work is good or bad, famous or forgotten. If circumstances neglect it, he congratulates himself, since he only wrote it to negate circumstances. But when a book that comes into being by chance, produced in a moment of idleness and lassitude, without value or significance, is suddenly made into a masterpiece by circumstantial events, what author is not going to take credit for the glory himself, in his heart of hearts, what author is not going to see his own worth in that glory, and his own work in that gift of fortune, the working of his mind in providential harmony with his time?

A writer is his own first dupe, and at the very moment he fools other people he is also fooling himself. Listen to him again: now he states that his function is to write for others, that as he writes he has nothing in mind but the reader's interest. He says this and he believes it. But it is not true at all. Because if he were not attentive first and foremost to what *he* is doing, if he were not concerned with literature as his own action, he could not even write: he would not be the one who was writing—the one writing would be no one. This is why it is futile for him to take the seriousness of an ideal as his guarantee, futile for him to claim to have stable values: this seriousness is not his own seriousness and can never settle definitively where he thinks he is. For example: he writes novels, and these novels imply certain political statements, so that he seems to side with a certain Cause. Other people, people who directly support the Cause, are then inclined to recognize him as one of themselves, to see his work as proof that the Cause is really his cause, but as soon as they make this claim, as soon as they try to become involved in this activity and take it over, they realize that the writer is not on their side, that he is only on his own side, that what interests him about the Cause is the operation he himself has carried out—and they are puzzled. It is easy to understand why men who have committed themselves to a party, who have made a decision, distrust writers who share their views; because these writers have also committed themselves to literature, and in the final analysis literature, by its very activity, denies the substance of what it represents. This is its law and its truth. If it renounces this in order to attach itself permanently to a truth outside itself, it ceases to be a litera- ture and the writer who still claims he is a writer enters into another aspect of bad faith. Then must a writer refuse to take an interest in anything, must he turn his face to the wall? The problem is that if he does this, his equivocation is just as great. First of all, looking at the wall is also turning towards the world; one is making the wall into the world. When a writer sinks into the pure intimacy of a work which is no one's business but his own, it may seem to other people—other writers and people involved in other activities—that at least they have been left at peace in their Thing and their own work. But not at all. The work created by this solitary person and enclosed in solitude contains within itself a point of view which concerns everyone, implicitly passing judg- ment on other works, on the problems of the times, becoming the accomplice of whatever it neglects, the enemy of whatever it abandons, and its indifference mingles hypocritically with everyone's passion.

What is striking is that in literature, deceit and mystification are not only inevitable but constitute the writer's honesty, whatever hope and truth are in him. Nowadays people often talk about the sickness of words, and we even become irritated with those who talk about it, and suspect them of making words sick so they can talk about it. This could be the case. The trouble is that this sickness is also the words' health. They may be torn apart by equivocation, but this equivocation is a good thing—without it there would be no dialogue. They may be falsified by misunderstanding—but this misunderstanding is the possibility of our understanding. They may be imbued with emptiness—but this empti- ness is their very meaning. Naturally, a writer can always make it his ideal to call a cat a cat. But what he cannot manage to do is then believe that he is on the way to health and sincerity. On the contrary, he is causing more mystification than ever, because the cat is not a cat, and anyone who claims that it is has nothing in mind but this hypocritical violence: Rolet is a rascal.[*]

There are many reasons for this imposture. We have just been discussing the first reason: literature is made up of different stages which are distinct from one another and in opposition to one another. Honesty, which is analytical because it tries to see clearly, separates these stages. Under the eyes of honesty pass in succession the author, the work, and the reader; in succession the art of writing, the thing written, and the truth of that thing or the Thing Itself; still in succession, the writer without a name, pure absence of himself, pure idleness, then the writer who is work, who is the action of a creation indifferent to what it is creating, then the writer who is the result of this work and is worth something because of this result and not because of the work, as real as the created thing is real; then the writer who is no longer affirmed by this result but denied by it, who saves the ephemeral work by saving its ideal, the truth of the work, etc. The writer is not simply one of these stages to the exclusion of the others, nor is he even all of them put together in their unimportant succession, but the action which brings them together and unifies them. As a result, when the honest conscience judges the writer by immobilizing him in one of these forms, when, for instance, it attempts to condemn the work because it is a failure, the writer's other honesty protests in the name of the other stages, in the name of the purity of art, which sees its own triumph in the failure—and likewise, every time a writer is challenged under one of his aspects he has no choice but to present himself as someone else, and when addressed as the author of a beautiful work, disown that work, and when admired as an inspiration and a genius, see in himself only application and hard work, and when read by everyone, say: "Who can read me? I haven't written anything." This shifting on the part of the writer makes him into someone who is perpetually absent, an irresponsible character without a

[*] Blanchot is referring to a remark made by Nicolas Boileau (1637-1711) in his first *Satire*: "J'appelle un chat un chat et Rolet un fripon" ("I call a cat a cat and Rolet a rascal"). Rolet was a notorious figure of the time. —*Tr.*

conscience, but this shifting also forms the extent of his presence, of his risks and his responsibility.

The trouble is that the writer is not only several people in one, but each stage of himself denies all the others, demands everything for itself alone and does not tolerate any conciliation or compromise. The writer must respond to several absolute and absolutely different commands at once, and his morality is made up of the confrontation and opposition of implacably hostile rules.

One rule says to him: "You will not write, you will remain nothingness, you will keep silent, you will not know words."

The other rule says: "Know nothing but words."

"Write to say nothing."

"Write to say something."

"No works; rather, the experience of yourself, the knowledge of what is unknown to you."

"A work! A real work, recognized by other people and important to other people."

"Obliterate the reader."

"Obliterate yourself before the reader."

"Write in order to be true."

"Write for the sake of truth."

"Then be a lie, because to write with truth in mind is to write what is not yet true and perhaps never will be true."

"It doesn't matter, write in order to act."

"Write—you who are afraid to act."

"Let freedom speak in you."

"Oh! do not let freedom become a word in you."

Which law should be obeyed? Which voice should be listened to? But the writer must listen to them all! What confusion! Isn't clarity his law? Yes, clarity too. He must therefore oppose himself, deny himself even as he affirms himself, look for the deepness of the night in the facility of the day, look in the shadows which never begin, to find the sure light which cannot end. He must save the world and be the abyss, justify existence and allow what does not exist to speak; he must be at the end of all eras in the universal plenitude, and he is the origin, the birth of what does nothing but come into being. Is he all that? Literature is all that, in him.

But isn't all that what literature would *like* to be, what in reality it is not? In that case, literature is nothing. But is it nothing?

Literature is not nothing. People who are contemptuous of literature are mistaken in thinking they are condemning it by saying it is nothing. "All that is only literature." This is how people create an opposition between action, which is a concrete initiative in the world, and the written word, which is supposed to be a passive expression on the surface of the world; people who are in favor of action reject literature, which does not act, and those in search of passion become writers so as not to act. But this is to condemn and to love in an abusive way. If we see work as the force of history, the force that transforms man while it transforms the world, then a writer's activity must be recognized as the highest form of work. When a man works, what does he do? He produces an object. That object is the realization of a plan which was unreal before then: it is the affirmation of a reality different from the elements which constitute it and it is the future of new objects, to the extent that it becomes a tool capable of creating other objects. For example, my project might be to get warm. As long as this project is only a desire, I can turn it over every possible way and still it will not make me warm. But now I build a stove: the stove transforms the empty ideal which was my desire into something real; it affirms the presence in the world of something which was not there before, and in so doing, denies something which was there before; before, I had in front of me stones and cast iron; now I no longer have either stones or cast iron, but instead the product of the transformation of these elements—that is, their denial and destruction—by work. Because of this object, the world is now different. All the more different because this stove will allow me to make other objects, which will in turn deny the former condition of the world and prepare its future. These objects, which I have produced by changing the state of things, will in turn change me. The idea of heat is nothing, but actual heat will make my life a different kind of life, and every new thing I am able to do from now on because of this heat will also make me someone different. Thus is history formed, say Hegel and Marx—by work which realizes being in denying it, and reveals it at the end of the negation.[5]

[5] Alexandre Kojève offers this interpretation of Hegel in his *Introduction à la lecture de Hegel* (*Leçons sur La Phénomenologie de l'Esprit*, selected and published by Raymond Queneau).

But what is a writer doing when he writes? Everything a man does when he works, but to an outstanding degree. The writer, too, produces something—a work in the highest sense of the word. He produces this work by transforming natural and human realities. When he writes, his starting point is a certain state of language, a certain form of culture, certain books, and also certain objective elements—ink, paper, printing presses. In order to write, he must destroy language in its present form and create it in another form, denying books as he forms a book out of what other books are not. This new book is certainly a reality: it can be seen, touched, even read. In any case, it is not nothing. Before I wrote it, I had an idea of it, at least I had the project of writing it, but I believe there is the same difference between that idea and the volume in which it is realized as between the desire for heat and the stove which makes me warm. For me, the written volume is an extraordinary, unforeseeable innovation—such that it is impossible for me to conceive what it is capable of being without writing it. This is why it seems to me to be an experiment whose effects I cannot grasp, no matter how consciously they were produced, and in the face of which I shall be unable to remain the same, for this reason: in the presence of something other, I become other. But there is an even more decisive reason: this other thing—the book—of which I had only an idea and which I could not possibly have known in advance, is precisely myself become other.

The book, the written thing, enters the world and carries out its work of transformation and negation. It, too, is the future of many other things, and not only books: by the projects which it can give rise to, by the undertakings it encourages, by the totality of the world of which it is a modified reflection, it is an infinite source of new realities, and because of these new realities existence will be something it was not before.

So is the book nothing? Then why should the act of building a stove pass for the sort of work which forms and produces history, and why should the act of writing seem like pure passivity which remains in the margins of history and which history produces in spite of itself? The question seems unreasonable, and yet it weighs on the writer and its weight is crushing. At first sight one has the impression that the formative power of written works is incomparably great; one has the impression that the writer is endowed with more power to act than anyone else since his actions are immeasurable, limitless: we know (or we like to believe) that one single work can change the course of the world. But this is precisely what makes us think twice. The influence authors exert is very great, it goes infinitely far beyond their actions, to such an extent that what is real in their actions does not carry over into their influence and that tiny bit of reality does not contain the real substance that the extent of their influence would require. What is an author capable of? Everything—first of all, everything: he is fettered, he is enslaved, but as long as he can find a few moments of freedom in which to write, he is *free* to create a world without slaves, a world in which the slaves become the masters and formulate a new law; thus, by writing, the chained man immediately obtains freedom for himself and for the world; he denies everything he is, in order to become everything he is not. In this sense, his work is a prodigious act, the greatest and most important there is. But let us examine this more closely. Insofar as he *immediately* gives himself the freedom he does not have, he is neglecting the actual conditions for his emancipation, he is neglecting to do the real thing that must be done so that the abstract idea of freedom can be realized. His negation is *global*. It not only negates his situation as a man who has been walled into prison but bypasses time that will open holes in these walls; it negates the negation of time, it negates the negation of limits. This is why this negation negates nothing, in the end, why the work in which it is realized is not a truly negative, destructive act of transformation, but rather the realization of the inability to negate anything, the refusal to take part in the world; it transforms the freedom which would have to be embodied in things in the process of time into an ideal above time, empty and inaccessible.

A writer's influence is linked to this privilege of being master of everything. But he is only master of everything, he possesses only the infinite; he lacks the finite, limit escapes him. Now, one cannot act in the infinite, one cannot accomplish anything in the unlimited, so that if a writer acts in quite a real way as he produces this real thing which is called a book, he is also discrediting all action by this action, because he is substituting for the world of determined things and defined work a world in which *everything* is *instantly* given and there is nothing left to do but read it and enjoy it.

In general, the writer seems to be subjected to a state of inactivity because he is the master of the imaginary, and those who follow him into the realm of the imaginary lose sight of the problems of their true lives. But the danger he represents is much more serious. The truth is that he ruins action, not because he deals with what is unreal but because he makes *all* of reality available to us. Unreality begins with the whole. The realm of the imaginary is not a strange region situated beyond the world, it is the world itself, but the world as entire, manifold, the world as a whole. That is why it is not in the world, because it is the world, grasped and realized in its entirety by the global negation of all the individual realities contained in it, by their disqualification, their absence, by the realization of that absence itself, which is how literary creation begins, for when literary creation goes back over each thing and each being, it cherishes the illusion that it is creating them, because now it is seeing and naming them from the starting point of *everything*, from the starting point of the *absence* of everything, that is, from nothing.

Certainly that literature which is said to be "purely imaginative" has its dangers. First of all, it is not pure imagination. It believes that it stands apart from everyday realities and actual events, but the truth is that it has stepped aside from them; it is that distance, that remove from the everyday which necessarily takes the everyday into consideration and describes it as separateness, as pure strangeness. What is more, it makes this distance into an absolute value, and then this separateness seems to be a source of general understanding, the capacity to grasp everything and attain everything immediately, for those who submit to its enchantment enough to emerge from both their life, which is nothing but limited understanding, and time, which is nothing but a narrow perspective. All this is the lie of a fiction. But this kind of literature has on its side the fact that it is not trying to deceive us: it presents itself as imaginary; it only puts to sleep those who want to go to sleep.

What is far more deceitful is the literature of action. It calls on people to do something. But if it wants to remain authentic literature, it must base its representation of this "something to do," this predetermined and specific goal, on a world where such an action turns back into the unreality of an abstract and absolute value. "Something to do," as it may be expressed in a work of literature, is never more than "everything remains to be done," whether it presents itself as this "everything," that is, as an absolute value, or whether it needs this "everything," into which it vanishes, to justify itself and prove that it has merit. The language of a writer, even if he is a revolutionary, is not the language of command. It does not command; it presents; and it does not present by causing whatever it portrays to be present, but by portraying it behind everything, as the meaning and the absence of this everything. The result is either that the appeal of the author to the reader is only an empty appeal, and expresses only the effort which a man cut off from the world makes to reenter the world, as he stands discreetly at its periphery—or that the "something to do," which can only be recovered by starting from absolute values, appears to the reader precisely as that which cannot be done or as that which requires neither work nor action in order to be done.

As we know, a writer's main temptations are called stoicism, scepticism, and the unhappy consciousness. These are all ways of thinking that a writer adopts for reasons he believes he has thought out carefully, but which only literature has thought out in him. A stoic: he is the man of the universe, which itself exists only on paper, and, a prisoner or a poor man, he endures his condition stoically because he can write and because the one minute of freedom in which he writes is enough to make him powerful and free, is enough to give him not his own freedom, which he derides, but universal freedom. A nihilist, because he does not simply negate this and that by methodical work which slowly transforms each thing: he negates everything at once, and he is obliged to negate everything, since he only deals with everything. The unhappy consciousness! It is only too evident that this unhappiness is his most profound talent, since he is a writer only by virture of his fragmented consciousness divided into irreconcilable moments called: inspiration—which negates all work; work—which negates the nothingness of genius; the ephemeral work—in which he creates himself by negating himself; the work as everything—in which he takes back from himself and from other people everything which he seems to give to himself and to them. But there is one other temptation.

Let us acknowledge that in a writer there is a movement which proceeds without pause, and almost without transition, from nothing to everything. Let us see in him that negation that is not satisfied with the unreality in which it exists, because it wishes to realize itself and can only do so by negating something real, more real than words, more true than the isolated individual in control: it therefore keeps urging him towards a worldly life and a public existence in order to induce him to conceive how, even as he writes, he can become that very existence. It is at this point that he encounters those decisive moments in history when everything seems put in question, when law, faith, the State, the world above, the world of the past—everything sinks effortlessly, without work, into nothingness. The man knows he has not stepped out of history, but history is now the void, the void in the process of realization; it is *absolute* freedom which has become an event. Such periods are given the name Revolution. At this moment, freedom aspires to be realized in the *immediate* form of *everything* is possible, everything can be done. A fabulous moment—and no one who has experienced it can completely recover from it, since he has experienced history as his own history and his own freedom as universal freedom. These moments are, in fact, fabulous moments: in them, fable speaks; in them, the speech of fable becomes action. That the writer should be tempted by them is completely appropriate. Revolutionary action is in every respect analogous to action as embodied in literature: the passage from nothing to everything, the affirmation of the absolute as event and of every event as absolute. Revolutionary action explodes with the same force and the same facility as the writer who has only to set down a few words side by side in order to change the world. Revolutionary action also has the same demand for purity, and the certainty that everything it does has absolute value, that it is not just any action performed to bring about some desirable and respectable goal, but that it is itself the ultimate goal, the Last Act. This last act is freedom, and the only choice left is between freedom and nothing. This is why, at that point, the only tolerable slogan is: *freedom or death*. Thus the Reign of Terror comes into being. People cease to be individuals working at specific tasks, acting here and only now: each person is universal freedom, and universal freedom knows nothing about elsewhere or tomorrow, or work or a work accomplished. At such times there is nothing left for anyone to do, because everything has been done. No one has a right to a private life any longer, everything is public, and the most guilty person is the suspect—the person who has a secret, who keeps a thought, an intimacy to himself. And in the end no one has a right to his life any longer, to his actually separate and physically distinct existence. This is the meaning of the Reign of Terror. Every citizen has a right to death, so to speak: death is not a sentence passed on him, it is his most essential right; he is not suppressed as a guilty person—he needs death so that he can proclaim himself a citizen and it is in the disappearance of death that freedom causes him to be born. Where this is concerned, the French Revolution has a clearer meaning than any other revolution. Death in the Reign of Terror is not simply a way of punishing seditionaries; rather, since it becomes the unavoidable, in some sense the desired lot of everyone, it appears as the very operation of freedom in free men. When the blade falls on Saint-Just and Robespierre, in a sense it executes no one. Robespierre's virtue, Saint-Just's relentlessness, are simply their existences already suppressed, the anticipated presence of their deaths, the decision to allow freedom to assert itself completely in them and through its universality negate the particular reality of their lives. Granted, perhaps they caused the Reign of Terror to take place. But the Terror they personify does not come from the death they inflict on others but from the death they inflict on themselves. They bear its features, they do their thinking and make their decisions with death sitting on their shoulders, and this is why their thinking is cold, implacable; it has the freedom of a decapitated head. The Terrorists are those who desire absolute freedom and are fully conscious that this constitutes a desire for their own death, they are conscious of the freedom they affirm, as they are conscious of their death which they realize, and consequently they behave during their lifetimes not like people living among other living people, but like beings deprived of being, like universal thoughts, pure abstractions beyond history, judging and deciding in the name of all of history.

Death as an event no longer has any importance. During the Reign of Terror individuals die and it means nothing. In the famous words of Hegel, "It is thus the coldest and meanest of all deaths, with no more significance than cutting off a head of cabbage or swallowing a mouthful of water."[6] Why? Isn't death the achievement of freedom—that is, the

[6] Hegel, *op. cit.*, p. 360.—*Tr.*

richest moment of meaning? But it is also only the empty point in that freedom, a manifestation of the fact that such a freedom is still abstract, ideal (literary), that it is only poverty and platitude. Each person dies, but everyone is alive, and that really also means everyone is dead. But "is dead" is the positive side of freedom which has become the world: here, being is revealed as absolute. "Dying," on the other hand, is pure insignificance, an event without concrete reality, one which has lost all value as a personal and interior drama, because there is no longer any interior. It is the moment when I die signifies to me as I die a banality which there is no way to take into consideration: in the liberated world and in these moments when freedom is an absolute apparition, dying is unimportant and death has no depth. The Reign of Terror and revolution—not war—have taught us this.

The writer sees himself in the Revolution. It attracts him because it is the time during which literature becomes history. It is his truth. Any writer who is not induced by the very fact of writing to think, "I am the revolution, only freedom allows me to write," is not really writing. In 1793 there is a man who identifies himself completely with revolution and the Reign of Terror. He is an aristocrat clinging to the battlements of his medieval castle, a tolerant man, rather shy and obsequiously polite: but he writes, all he does is write, and it doesn't matter that freedom puts him back into the Bastille after having brought him out, he is the one who understands freedom the best, because he understands that it is a time when the most insane passions can turn into political realities, a time when they have a right to be seen, and are the law. He is also the man for whom death is the greatest passion and the ultimate platitude, who cuts off people's heads the way you cut a head of cabbage, with such great indifference that nothing is more unreal than the death he inflicts, and yet no one has been more acutely aware that death is sovereign, that freedom is death. Sade is the writer *par excellence,* he combines all the writer's contradictions. Alone: of all men he is the most alone, and yet at the same time a public figure and an important political personage; forever locked up and yet absolutely free, theoretician and symbol of absolute freedom. He writes a vast body of work, and that work exists for no one. Unknown: but what he portrays has an immediate significance for everyone. He is nothing more than a writer, and he depicts life raised to the level of a passion, a passion which has become cruelty and madness. He turns the most bizarre, the most hidden, the most unreasonable kind of feeling into a universal affirmation, the reality of a public statement which is consigned to history to become a legitimate explanation of man's general condition. He is, finally, negation itself: his *oeuvre* is nothing but the work of negation, his experience the action of a furious negation, driven to blood, denying other people, denying God, denying nature and, within this circle in which it runs endlessly, reveling in itself as absolute sovereignty.

Literature contemplates itself in revolution, it finds its justification in revolution, and if it has been called the Reign of Terror, this is because its ideal is indeed that moment in history, that moment when "life endures death and maintains itself in it" in order to gain from death the possibility of speaking and the truth of speech. This is the "question" that seeks to pose itself in literature, the "question" that is its essence. Literature is bound to language. Language is reassuring and disquieting at the same time. When we speak, we gain control over things with satisfying ease. I say, "This woman," and she is immediately available to me, I push her away, I bring her close, she is everything I want her to be, she becomes the place in which the most surprising sorts of transformations occur and actions unfold: speech is life's ease and security. We can't do anything with an object that has no name. Primitive man knows that the possession of words gives him mastery over things, but for him the relationship between words and the world is so close that the manipulation of language is as difficult and as fraught with peril as contact with living beings: the name has not emerged from the thing, it is the inside of the thing which has been dangerously brought out into the open and yet it is still the hidden depths of the thing; the thing has therefore not yet been named. The more closely man becomes attached to a civilization, the more he can manipulate words with innocence and composure. Is it that words have lost all relation to what they designate? But this absence of relation is not a defect, and if it is a defect, this defect is the only thing that gives language its full value, so that of all languages the most perfect is the language of mathematics, which is spoken in a rigorous way and to which no entity corresponds.

I say, "This woman." Hölderlin, Mallarmé, and all poets whose theme is the essence of poetry have felt that the act of naming is disquieting and marvellous. A word may give me its meaning, but first it suppresses it. For me to be able to say, "This woman" I must somehow take her flesh and blood reality away from her, cause her to be absent, annihilate her. The word gives me the being, but it gives it to me deprived of being. The word is the absence of that being, its nothingness, what is left of it when it has lost being—the very fact that it does not exist. Considered in this light, speaking is a curious right. In a text dating from before *The Phenomenology*, Hegel, here the friend and kindred spirit of Hölderlin, writes: "Adam's first act, which made him master of the animals, was to give them names, that is, he annihilated them in their existence (as existing creatures)."[7] Hegel means that from that moment on the cat ceased to be a uniquely real cat and became an idea as well. The meaning of speech, then, requires that before any word is spoken there must be a sort of immense hecatomb, a preliminary flood plunging all of creation into a total sea. God had created living things, but man had to annihilate them. Not until then did they take on meaning for him, and he in turn created them out of the death into which they had disappeared; only instead of beings (*êtres*) and, as we say, existants (*existants*), there remained only being (*l'être*), and man was condemned not to be able to approach anything or experience anything except through the meaning he had to create. He saw that he was enclosed in daylight, and he knew this day could not end, because the end itself was light, since it was from the end of beings that their meaning—which is being—had come.

Of course my language does not kill anyone. And yet: when I say, "This woman," real death has been announced and is already present in my language; my language means that this person, who is here right now, can be detached from herself, removed from her existence and her presence and suddenly plunged into a nothingness in which there is no existence or presence; my language essentially signifies the possibility of this destruction; it is a constant, bold allusion to such an event. My

---

[7] From a collection of essays entitled *System of 1803-1804*. A. Kojève, in his *Introduction à la lecture de Hegel*, interpreting a passage from *The Phenomenology*, demonstrates in a remarkable way how for Hegel comprehension was equivalent to murder.

language does not kill anyone. But if this woman were not really capable of dying, if she were not threatened by death at every moment of her life, bound and joined to death by an essential bond, I would not be able to carry out that ideal negation, that deferred assassination which is what my language is.

Therefore it is accurate to say that when I speak: death speaks in me. My speech is a warning that at this very moment death is loose in the world, that it has suddenly appeared between me, as I speak, and the being I address: it is there between us as the distance that separates us, but this distance is also what prevents us from being separated, because it contains the condition for all understanding. Death alone allows me to grasp what I want to attain; it exists in words as the only way they can have meaning. Without death, everything would sink into absurdity and nothingness.

This situation has various consequences. Clearly, in me, the power to speak is also linked to my absence from being. I say my name, and it is as though I were chanting my own dirge: I separate myself from myself, I am no longer either my presence or my reality, but an objective, impersonal presence, the presence of my name, which goes beyond me and whose stone-like immobility performs exactly the same function for me as a tombstone weighing on the void. When I speak, I deny the existence of what I am saying, but I also deny the existence of the person who is saying it: if my speech reveals being in its nonexistence, it also affirms that this revelation is made on the basis of the nonexistence of the person making it, out of his power to remove himself from himself, to be other than his being. This is why, if true language is to begin, the life that will carry this language must have experienced its nothingness, must have "trembled in the depths; and everything in it that was fixed and stable must have been shaken." Language can only begin with the void; no fullness, no certainty can ever speak; something essential is lacking in anyone who expresses himself. Negation is tied to language. When I first begin, I do not speak in order to say something, rather a nothing demands to speak, nothing speaks, nothing finds its being in speech and the being of speech is nothing. This formulation explains why literature's ideal has been the following: to say nothing, to speak in order to say nothing. That is not the musing of a high-class kind of nihilism.

Language perceives that its meaning derives not from what exists, but from its own retreat before existence, and it is tempted to proceed no further than this retreat, to try to attain negation in itself and to make everything of nothing. If one is not to talk about things except to say what makes them nothing, well then, to say nothing is really the only hope of saying everything about them.

A hope which is naturally problematic. Everyday language calls a cat a cat, as if the living cat and its name were identical, as if it were not true that when we name the cat we retain nothing of it but its absence, what it is not. Yet for a moment everyday language is right, in that even if the word excludes the existence of what it designates, it still refers to it through the thing's nonexistence, which has become its essence. To name the cat is, if you like, to make it into a non-cat, a cat that has ceased to exist, has ceased to be a living cat, but this does not mean one is making it into a dog, or even a non-dog. That is the primary difference between common language and literary language. The first accepts that once the nonexistence of the cat has passed into the word, the cat itself comes to life again fully and certainly in the form of its idea (its being) and its meaning: on the level of being (idea), the word restores to the cat all the certainty it had on the level of existence. And in fact that certainty is even much greater: things can change if they have to, sometimes they stop being what they are—they remain hostile, unavailable, inaccessible; but the being of these things, their idea, does not change: the idea is definitive, it is sure, we even call it eternal. Let us hold on to words, then, and not revert back to things, let us not let go of words, not believe they are sick. Then we'll be at peace.

Common language is probably right, this is the price we pay for our peace. But literary language is made of uneasiness; it is also made of contradictions. Its position is not very stable or secure. On the one hand, its only interest in a thing is in the meaning of the thing, its absence, and it would like to attain this absence absolutely in itself and for itself, to grasp in its entirety the infinite movement of comprehension. What is more, it observes that the word cat is not only the nonexistence of the cat, but a nonexistence made *word*, that is, a completely determined and objective reality. It sees that there is a difficulty and even a lie in this. How can it hope to have achieved what it set out to do, since it has transposed the unreality of the thing into the reality of language? How could the infinite absence of comprehension consent to be confused with the limited, restricted presence of a single word? And isn't everyday language mistaken when it tries to persuade us of this? In fact, it is deceiving itself and it is deceiving us, too. Speech is not sufficient for the truth it contains. Take the trouble to listen to a single word: in that word, nothingness is struggling and toiling away, it digs tirelessly, doing its utmost to find a way out, nullifying what encloses it—it is infinite disquiet, formless and nameless vigilance. Already the seal which held this nothingness within the limits of the word and within the guise of its meaning has been broken; now there is access to other names, names which are less fixed, still vague, more capable of adapting to the savage freedom of the negative essence—they are unstable groups, no longer terms, but the movement of terms, an endless sliding of "turns of phrase" which do not lead anywhere. Thus is born the image that does not directly designate the thing, but rather, what the thing is not; it speaks of a dog instead of a cat. This is how the pursuit begins in which all of language, in motion, is asked to give in to the uneasy demands of one single thing that has been deprived of being and that, after having wavered between each word, tries to lay hold of them all again in order to negate them all at once, so that they will designate the void as they sink down into it—this void which they can neither fill nor represent.

Even if literature stopped here, it would have a strange and embarassing job to do. But it does not stop here. It recalls the first name which would be the murder Hegel speaks of. The "existant" was called out of its existence by the word and it became being. This *Lazare, veni foras* summoned the dark cadaverous reality from its primordial depths and in exchange gave it only the life of the mind. Language knows that its kingdom is day and not the intimacy of the unrevealed; it knows that in order for the day to begin, for the day to be that Orient which Hölderlin glimpsed—not light that has become the repose of noon, but the terrible force that draws beings into the world and illuminates them— something must be left out. Negation cannot be created out of anything but the reality of what it is negating; language derives its value and its pride from the fact that it is the achievement of this negation; but in the beginning, what was lost? The torment of language is what it lacks because of the necessity that it be the lack of precisely this. It cannot even name it.

Whoever sees God dies. In speech what dies is what gives life to speech; speech is the life of that death, it is "the life that endures death and maintains itself in it." What wonderful power. But something was there and is no longer there. Something has disappeared. How can I recover it, how can I turn around and look at what exists *before*, if all my power consists of making it into what exists *after*? The language of literature is a search for this moment which precedes literature. Literature usually calls it existence; it wants the cat as it exists, the pebble *taking the side of things*, not man, but the pebble, and in this pebble what man rejects by saying it, what is the foundation of speech and what speech excludes in speaking, the abyss, Lazarus in the tomb and not Lazarus brought back into the daylight, the one who already smells bad, who is Evil, Lazarus lost and not Lazarus saved and brought back to life. *I say a flower!* But in the absence where I mention it, through the oblivion to which I relegate the image it gives me, in the depths of this heavy word, itself looming up like an unknown thing, I passionately summon the darkness of this flower, I summon this perfume that passes through me though I do not breathe it, this dust that impregnates me though I do not see it, this color which is a trace and not light. Then what hope do I have of attaining the thing I push away? My hope lies in the materiality of language, in the fact that words are things, too, are a kind of nature—this is given to me and gives me more than I can understand. Just now the reality of words was an obstacle. Now, it is my only chance. A name ceases to be the ephemeral passing of nonexistence and becomes a concrete ball, a solid mass of existence; language, abandoning the sense, the meaning which was all it wanted to be, tries to become senseless. Everything physical takes precedence: rhythm, weight, mass, shape, and then the paper on which one writes, the trail of the ink, the book. Yes, happily language is a thing: it is a written thing, a bit of bark, a sliver of rock, a fragment of clay in which the reality of the earth continues to exist. The word acts not as an ideal force but as an obscure power, as an incantation that coerces things, makes them *really* present outside of themselves. It is an element, a piece barely detached from its subterranean surroundings: it is no longer a name, but rather one moment in the universal anonymity, a bald statement, the stupor of a confrontation in the depths of obscurity. And in this way language insists on playing its own game without man, who created it. Literature now dispenses with the writer: it is no longer this inspiration at work, this negation asserting itself, this idea inscribed in the world as though it were the absolute perspective of the world in its totality. It is not beyond the world, but neither is it the world itself: it is the presence of things before the *world* exists, their perseverance after the world has disappeared, the stubbornness of what remains when everything vanishes and the dumbfoundedness of what appears when nothing exists. That is why it cannot be confused with consciousness, which illuminates things and makes decisions; it is *my* consciousness *without me*, the radiant passivity of mineral substances, the lucidity of the depths of torpor. It is not the night; it is the obsession of the night; it is not the night, but the consciousness of the night, which lies awake watching for a chance to surprise itself and because of that is constantly being dissipated. It is not the day, it is the side of the day that day has rejected in order to become light. And it is not death either, because it manifests existence without being, existence which remains below existence, like an inexorable affirmation, without beginning or end—death as the impossibility of dying.

By turning itself into an inability to reveal anything, literature is attempting to become the revelation of what revelation destroys. This is a tragic endeavor. Literature says: "I no longer represent, I am; I do not signify, I present." But this wish to be a thing, this refusal to mean anything, a refusal immersed in words turned to salt; in short, this destiny which literature becomes as it becomes the language of no one, the writing of no writer, the light of a consciousness deprived of self, this insane effort to bury itself in itself, to hide itself behind the fact that it is visible—all this is what literature now manifests, what literature now shows. If it were to become as mute as a stone, as passive as the corpse enclosed behind that stone, its decision to lose the capacity for speech would still be legible on the stone and would be enough to wake that bogus corpse.

Literature learns that it cannot go beyond itself towards its own end: it hides, it does not give itself away. It knows it is the movement through which whatever disappears keeps appearing. When it names something, whatever it designates is abolished; but whatever is abolished is also sustained, and the thing has found a refuge (in the being which is the word) rather than a threat. When literature refuses to name anything, when it turns a name into something obscure and meaningless, witness to the primordial obscurity, what has disappeared in this case—the meaning of the name—is really destroyed, but signification in general has appeared in its place, the meaning of the meaninglessness embedded in the word as expression of the obscurity of existence, so that although the precise meaning of the terms has faded, what asserts itself now is the very possibility of signifying, the empty power of bestowing meaning—a strange impersonal light.

By negating the day, literature recreates day in the form of fatality; by affirming the night, it finds the night as the impossibility of the night. This is its discovery. When day is the light of the world, it illuminates what it lets us see: it is the capacity to grasp, to live, it is the answer "understood" in every question. But if we call the day to account, if we reach a point where we push it away in order to find out what is prior to the day, under it, we discover that the day is already present, and that what is prior to the day is still the day, but in the form of an inability to disappear, not a capacity to make something appear: the darkness of necessity, not the light of freedom. The nature, then, of what is prior to the day, of prediurnal existence, is the dark side of the day, and that dark side is not the undisclosed mystery of its beginning, but its inevitable presence—the statement "There is no day," which merges with "There is already day," its appearance coinciding with the moment when it has not yet appeared. In the course of the day, the day allows us to escape from things, it lets us comprehend them, and as it lets us comprehend them, it makes them transparent and as if null—but what we cannot escape from is the day: within it we are free, but it, itself, is fatality, and day in the form of fatality is the being of what is prior to the day, the existence we must turn away from in order to speak and comprehend.

If one looks at it in a certain way, literature has two slopes. One side of literature is turned toward the movement of negation by which things are separated from themselves and destroyed in order to be known, subjugated, communicated. Literature is not content to accept only the fragmentary, successive results of this movement of negation: it wants to grasp the movement itself and it wants to comprehend the results in their totality. If negation is assumed to have gotten control of everything, then real things, taken one by one, all refer back to that unreal whole which they form together, to the world which is their meaning as a group, and this is the point of view that literature has adopted—it looks at things from the point of view of this still *imaginary* whole which they would *really* constitute if negation could be achieved. Hence its non-realism—the shadow which is its prey. Hence its distrust of words, its need to apply the movement of negation to language itself and to exhaust it by realizing it as that totality on the basis of which each term would be nothing.

But there is another side to literature. Literature is a concern for the reality of things, for their unknown, free, and silent existence; literature is their innocence and their forbidden presence, it is the being which protests against revelation, it is the defiance of what does not want to take place outside. In this way, it sympathizes with darkness, with aimless passion, with lawless violence, with everything in the world that seems to perpetuate the refusal to come into the world. In this way, too, it allies itself with the reality of language, it makes language into matter without contour, content without form, a force that is capricious and impersonal and says nothing, reveals nothing, simply announces—through its refusal to say anything—that it comes from night and will return to night. In itself, this metamorphosis is not unsuccessful. It is certainly true that words are transformed. They no longer *signify* shadow, earth, they no longer represent the absence of shadow and earth which is meaning, which is the shadow's light, which is the transparency of the earth: opacity is their answer; the flutter of closing wings is their speech; in them, physical weight is present as the stifling density of an accumulation of syllables that has lost all meaning. The metamorphosis has taken place. But beyond the change that has solidified, petrified, and stupefied words two things reappear in this metamorphosis: the meaning of this metamorphosis, which illuminates the words, and the meaning the words contain by virtue of their apparition as things or, if it should happen this way, as vague, indeterminate, elusive existences in which nothing appears, the heart of depth without appearance. Literature has certainly triumphed over the meaning of words, but what it has found in words considered apart from their meaning is meaning that has become thing: and thus it is meaning detached from its conditions, separated from its moments, wandering like an empty power, a power no one can do anything with, a power without power, the simple inability to cease to be, but which, because of that, appears to be the proper determination of indeterminate and meaningless existence. In this endeavor, literature does not confine itself to rediscovering in the interior what it tried to leave behind on the threshold. Because what it finds, as the interior, is the outside which has been changed from the outlet it once was into the impossibility of going out—and what it finds as the darkness of existence is the being of day which has been changed from explicatory light, creative of meaning, into the aggravation of what one cannot prevent oneself from understanding and the stifling obsession of a reason without any principle, without any beginning, which one cannot account for. Literature is that experience through which the consciousness discovers its being in its inability to lose consciousness, in the movement whereby, as it disappears, as it tears itself away from the meticulousness of an I, it is recreated beyond unconsciousness as an impersonal spontaneity, the desperate eagerness of a haggard knowledge which knows nothing, which no one knows, and which ignorance always discovers behind itself as its own shadow changed into a gaze.

One can, then, accuse language of having become an interminable resifting of words, instead of the silence it wanted to achieve. Or one can complain that it has immersed itself in the conventions of literature when what it wanted was to be absorbed into existence. That is true. But this endless resifting of words without content, this continuousness of speech through an immense pillage of words, is precisely the profound nature of a silence that talks even in its dumbness, a silence that is speech empty of words, an echo speaking on and on in the midst of silence. And in the same way literature, a blind vigilance which in its attempt to escape from itself plunges deeper and deeper into its own obsession, is the only rendering of the obsession of existence, if this itself is the very impossibility of emerging from existence, if it is being which is always flung back into being, that which in the bottomless depth is already at the bottom of the abyss, a recourse against which there is no recourse. [8]

Literature is divided between these two slopes. The problem is that even though they are apparently incompatible they do not lead toward distinctly different works or goals, and that an art which purports to follow one slope is already on the other. The first slope is meaningful prose. Its goal is to express things in a language that designates things according to what they mean. This is the way everyone speaks; and many people write the way we speak. But still on this side of language, there comes a moment when art realizes that everyday speech is dishonest and abandons it. What is art's complaint about everyday speech? It says it lacks meaning: art feels it is madness to think that in each word some thing is completely present through the absence that determines it, and so art sets off in quest of a language that can recapture this absence itself and represent the endless movement of comprehension. We do not need to discuss this position again, we have described it at length already. But what can be said about this kind of art? That it is a search for a pure form, that it is a vain preoccupation with empty words? Quite the contrary: its only concern is true meaning; its only preoccupation is to safeguard the movement by which this meaning becomes truth. To be fair, we must consider it more significant than any ordinary prose, which only subsists on false meanings: it represents the world for us, it teaches us to discover the total being of the world, it is the work of the negative in the world and for the world. How can we help admiring it as preeminently active, lively and lucid art? Of course we must. But then we must appreciate the same qualities in Mallarmé, who is the master of this art.

Mallarmé is on the other slope of literature, too. In some sense all the people we call poets come together on that slope. Why? Because they

---

[8] In his book De l'existence à l'existant, Emmanuel Lévinas uses the term il y a ["there is"] to throw some "light" on this anonymous and impersonal flow of being that precedes all being, being that is already present in the heart of disappearance, that in the depths of annihilation still returns to being, being as the fatality of being, nothingness as existence: when there is nothing, il y a being. See also Deucalion I. [Existence and Existents, tr. A. Lingis, Kluwer, Boston, 1978. —Tr.]

are interested in the reality of language, because they are not interested in the world, but in what things and beings would be if there were no world; because they devote themselves to literature as to an impersonal power that only wants to be engulfed and submerged. If this is what poetry is like, at least we will know why it must be withdrawn from history, where it produces a strange insect-like buzzing in the margins, and we will also know that no work which allows itself to slip down this slope towards the chasm can be called a work of prose. Well, what is it then? Everyone understands that literature cannot be divided up and that if you choose exactly where your place in it is, if you convince yourself that you really are where you wanted to be, you risk becoming very confused, because literature has already insidiously caused you to pass from one slope to the other and changed you into something you were not before. This is its treachery; this is also its cunning version of the truth. A novelist writes in the most transparent kind of prose, he describes men we could have met ourselves and actions we could have performed; he says his aim is to express the reality of a human world the way Flaubert did. In the end, though, his work really has only one subject. What is it? The horror of existence deprived of the world, the process through which whatever ceases to be continues to be, whatever is forgotten is always answerable to memory, whatever dies encounters only the impossibility of dying, whatever seeks to attain the beyond is always still here. This *process* is day which has become fatality, consciousness whose light is no longer the lucidity of the vigil but the stupor of lack of sleep, it is existence without being, as poetry tries to recapture it behind the meaning of words, which reject it.

Now here is a man who does more observing than writing: he walks in a pine forest, looks at a wasp, picks up a stone. He is a sort of scholar, but this scholar fades away in the face of what he knows, sometimes in the face of what he wants to know; he is a man who learns for the sake of other men: he has gone over to the side of objects, sometimes he is water, sometimes a pebble, sometimes a tree, and when he observes things, he does it for the sake of things, and when he describes something, it is the thing itself that describes itself. Now, this is the surprising aspect of the transformation, because no doubt it is possible to become a tree, and is there any writer who could not succeed in making a tree talk?

But Francis Ponge's tree is a tree that has observed Francis Ponge and that describes itself as it imagines Ponge might describe it. These are strange descriptions. Certain traits make them seem completely human: the fact is that the tree knows the weakness of men who only speak about what they know; but all these metaphors borrowed from the picturesque human world, these images which form an image, really represent the way things regard man, they really represent the singularity of human speech animated by the life of the cosmos and the power of seeds; this is why other things slip in among these images, among certain objective notions—because the tree knows that science is a common ground of understanding between the two worlds: what slip in are vague recollections rising from deep down in the earth, expressions that are in the process of metamorphosing, words in which a thick fluidity of vegetable growth insinuates itself under the clear meaning. Doesn't everyone think he understands these descriptions, written in perfectly meaningful prose? Doesn't everyone think they belong to the clear and human side of literature? And yet they do not belong to the world but to the underside of the world; they do not attest to form but to lack of form, and they are only clear to a person who does not penetrate them, the opposite of the oracular words of the tree of Dodona—another tree—which were obscure but concealed a meaning: these are clear only because they hide their lack of meaning. Indeed, Ponge's descriptions begin at that hypothetical moment after the world has been achieved, history completed, nature almost made human, when speech advances to meet the thing and the thing learns to speak. Ponge captures this touching moment when existence, which is still mute, encounters speech at the edge of the world, speech which as we know is the murderer of existence. From the depths of dumbness, he hears the striving of an antediluvian language and he recognizes the profound work of the elements in the clear speech of the concept. In this way he becomes the will that mediates between that which is rising slowly to speech and speech which is descending slowly to the earth, expressing not existence as it was before the day, but existence as it is after the day: the world of the end of the world.

Where in a work lies the beginning of the moment when the words become stronger than their meaning and the meaning more physical than the word? When does Lautréamont's prose lose the name of prose?

Isn't each sentence understandable? Isn't each group of sentences logical? And don't the words say what they mean? At what moment, in this labyrinth of order, in this maze of clarity, did meaning stray from the path? At what turning did reason become aware that it had stopped "following," that something else was continuing, progressing, concluding in its place, something like it in every way, something reason thought it recognized as itself, until the moment it woke up and discovered this other that had taken its place? But if reason now retraces its steps in order to denounce the intruder, the illusion immediately vanishes into thin air, reason finds only itself there, the prose is prose again, so that reason starts off again and loses its way again, allowing a sickening physical substance to replace it, something like a walking staircase, a corridor that unfolds ahead—a kind of reason whose infallibility excludes all reasoners, a logic that has become the "logic of things." Then where is the work? Each moment has the clarity of a beautiful language being spoken, but the work as a whole has the opaque meaning of a thing that is being eaten and that is also eating, that is devouring, being swallowed up and recreating itself in a vain effort to change itself into nothing.

Lautréamont is not a true writer of prose? But what is Sade's style, if it isn't prose? And does anyone write more clearly than he does? Is there anyone less familiar than he—who grew up in the least poetic century—with the preoccupations of a literature in search of obscurity? And yet in what other work do we hear such an impersonal, inhuman sound, such a "gigantic and haunting murmur" (as Jean Paulhan says)? But this is simply a defect! The weakness of a writer who cannot be brief! It is certainly a serious defect—literature is the first to accuse him of it. But what it condemns on one side becomes a merit on the other; what it denounces in the name of the work it admires as an experience; what seems unreadable is really the only thing worth being written. And at the end of everything is fame; beyond, there is oblivion; farther beyond, anonymous survival as part of a dead culture; even farther beyond, perseverance in the eternity of the elements. Where is the end? Where is that death which is the hope of language? But language is *the life that endures death and maintains itself in it.*

If we want to restore literature to the movement which allows all its ambiguities to be grasped, that movement is here: literature, like ordinary speech, *begins* with the *end*, which is the only thing that allows us to understand. If we are to speak, we must see death, we must see it behind us. When we speak, we are leaning on a tomb, and the void of that tomb is what makes language true, but at the same time void is reality and death becomes being. There is being—that is to say, a logical and expressible truth—and there is a world, because we can destroy things and suspend existence. This is why we can say that there is being because there is nothingness: death is man's possibility, his chance, it is through death that the future of a finished world is still there for us; death is man's greatest hope, his only hope of being man. This is why existence is his only real dread, as Emmanuel Lévinas has clearly shown,[9] existence frightens him, not because of death which could put an end to it, but because it excludes death, because it is still there underneath death, a presence in the depths of absence, an inexorable day in which all days rise and set. And there is no question that we are preoccupied by dying. But why? It is because when we die, we leave behind not only the world but also death. That is the paradox of the last hour. Death works with us in the world; it is a power that humanizes nature, that raises existence to being, and it is within each one of us as our most human quality; it is death only in the world—man only knows death because he is man, and he is only man because he is death in the process of becoming. But to die is to shatter the world; it is the loss of the person, the annihilation of the being; and so it is also the loss of death, the loss of what in it and for me made it death. As long as I live, I am a mortal man, but when I die, by ceasing to be a man I also cease to be mortal, I am no longer capable of dying, and my impending death horrifies me because I see it as it is: no longer death, but the impossibility of dying.

Certain religions have taken the impossibility of death and called it immortality. That is, they have tried to "humanize" the very event which signifies: "I cease to be a man." But it is only the opposite thrust

---

[9] He writes, "Isn't dread in the face of being—horror of being—just as primordial as dread in the face of death? Isn't fear of being just as primordial as fear for one's being? Even more primordial, because one could account for the latter by means of the former." (*De l'existence à l'existant*)

that makes death impossible: through death I lose the advantage of being mortal, because I lose the possibility of being man; to be man beyond death could only have this strange meaning—to be, in spite of death, still capable of dying, to go on as though nothing had happened, with death as a horizon and the same hope—death which would have no outcome beyond a "go on as though nothing had happened," etc. This is what other religions have called the curse of being reborn: you die, but you die badly because you have lived badly, you are condemned to live again, and you live again until, having become a man completely, in dying you become a truly blessed man—a man who is really dead. Kafka inherited this idea from the Kabbalah and Eastern traditions. A man enters the night, but the night ends in awakening, and there he is, an insect. Or else the man dies, but he is actually alive; he goes from city to city, carried along by rivers, recognized by some people, helped by no one, the mistake made by old death snickering at his bedside; his is a strange condition, he has forgotten to die. But another man thinks he is alive, the fact is he has forgotten his death, and yet another, knowing he is dead, struggles in vain to die; death is over there, the great unattainable castle, and life was over there, the native land he left in answer to a false summons; now there is nothing to do but to struggle, to work at dying completely, but if you struggle you are still alive; and everything that brings the goal closer also makes the goal inaccessible.

Kafka did not make this theme the expression of a drama about the next world, but he did try to use it to capture the present fact of our condition. He saw in literature the best way of trying to find a way out for this condition, not only of describing it. This is high praise, but does literature deserve it? It is true that there is powerful trickery in literature, a mysterious bad faith that allows it to play everything both ways and gives the most honest people an unreasonable hope of losing and yet winning at the same time. First of all, literature, too, is working towards the advent of the world; literature is civilization and culture. In this way, it is already uniting two contradictory movements. It is negation, because it drives the inhuman, indeterminate side of things back into nothingness; it defines them, makes them finite, and this is the sense in which literature is really the work of death in the world. But at the same time, after having denied things in their existence, it preserves them in their being; it causes things to have a meaning, and the negation which is death at work is also the advent of meaning, the activity of comprehension. Besides this, literature has a certain privilege: it goes beyond the immediate place and moment, and situates itself at the edge of the world and as if at the end of time, and it is from this position that it speaks about things and concerns itself with men. From this new power, literature apparently gains a superior authority. By revealing to each moment the whole of which it is a part, literature helps it to be aware of the whole that it is not and to become another moment that will be a moment within another whole, and so forth; because of this, literature can be called the greatest ferment in history. But there is one inconvenient consequence: this whole which literature represents is not simply an idea, since it is *realized* and not formulated abstractly—but it is not realized in an objective way, because what is real in it is not the whole but the particular language of a particular work, which is itself immersed in history; what is more, the whole does not present itself as real, but as fictional, that is, precisely as whole, as everything: perspective of the world, grasp of that *imaginary* point where the world can be seen in its entirety. What we are talking about, then, is a view of the world which realizes itself as unreal using language's peculiar reality. Now, what is the consequence of this? As for the task which is the world, literature is now regarded more as a bother than as a serious help; it is not the result of any true work, since it is not reality but the realization of a point of view which remains unreal; it is foreign to any true culture, because culture is the work of a person changing himself little by little over a period of time, and not the immediate enjoyment of a fictional transformation which dispenses with both time and work.

Spurned by history, literature plays a different game. If it is not really in the world, working to make the world, this is because its lack of being (of intelligible reality) causes it to refer to an existence that is still inhuman. Yes, it recognizes that this is so, that in its nature there is a strange slipping back and forth between being and not being, presence and absence, reality and nonreality. What is a work? Real words and an imaginary story, a world in which everything that happens is borrowed from reality, and this world is inaccessible; characters who are portrayed as living—but we know that their life consists of not living (of remaining a fiction); pure nothingness, then? But the book is there and we can touch it, we read the words and we can't change them; is it the nothingness of an idea, then, of something which exists only when understood? But the fiction is not understood, it is experienced through the words with which it is realized, and for me, as I read it or write it, it is more real than many real events, because it is impregnated with all the reality of language and it substitutes itself for my life simply by existing. Literature does not act: but what it does is plunge into this depth of existence which is neither being nor nothingness and where the hope of doing anything is completely eliminated. It is not explanation, and it is not pure comprehension, because the inexplicable emerges in it. And it expresses without expressing, it offers its language to what is murmured in the absence of speech. So literature seems to be allied with the strangeness of that existence which being has rejected and which does not fit into any category. The writer senses that he is in the grasp of an impersonal power that does not let him either live or die: the irresponsibility he cannot surmount becomes the expression of that death without death which awaits him at the edge of nothingness; literary immortality is the very movement by which the nausea of a survival which is not a survival, a death which does not end anything, insinuates itself into the world, a world sapped by crude existence. The writer who writes a work eliminates himself as he writes that work and at the same time affirms himself in it. If he has written it to get rid of himself, it turns out that the work engages him and recalls him to himself, and if he writes it to reveal himself and live in it, he sees that what he has done is nothing, that the greatest work is not as valuable as the most insignificant act, and that his work condemns him to an existence that is not his own existence and to a life that has nothing to do with life. Or again he has written because in the depths of language he heard the work of death as it prepared living beings for the truth of their name: he worked for this nothingness and he himself was a nothingness at work. But as one realizes the void, one creates a work, and the work, born of fidelity to death, is in the end no longer capable of dying; and all it brings to the person who was trying to prepare an unstoried death for himself is the mockery of immortality.

Then where is literature's power? It plays at working in the world, and the world regards its work as a worthless or dangerous game. It opens a path for itself towards the obscurity of existence and does not succeed in pronouncing the "Never more" which would suspend its curse. Then where is its force? Why would a man like Kafka decide that if he had to fall short of his destiny, being a writer was the only way to fall short of it truthfully. Perhaps this is an unintelligible enigma, but if it is, the source of the mystery is literature's right to affix a negative or positive sign indiscriminately to each of its moments and each of its results. A strange right—one linked to the question of ambiguity in general. Why is there ambiguity in the world? Ambiguity is its own answer. We can't answer it except by rediscovering it in the ambiguity of our answer, and an ambiguous answer is a question about ambiguity. One of the ways it reduces us is by making us want to clear it up, a struggle that is like the struggle against evil Kafka talks about, which ends in evil, "like the struggle with women, which ends in bed."

Literature is language turning into ambiguity. Ordinary language is not necessarily clear, it does not always say what it says; misunderstanding is also one of its paths. This is inevitable. Every time we speak we make words into monsters with two faces, one being reality, physical presence, and the other meaning, ideal absence. But ordinary language limits equivocation. It solidly encloses the absence in a presence, it puts *a term* to understanding, to the indefinite movement of comprehension; understanding is limited, but misunderstanding is limited, too. In literature, ambiguity is in some sense abandoned to its excesses by the opportunities it finds and exhausted by the extent of the abuses it can commit. It is as though there were a hidden trap here to force ambiguity to reveal its own traps, and as though in surrendering unreservedly to ambiguity literature were attempting to keep it—out of sight of the world and out of the thought of the world—in a place where it fulfills itself without endangering anything. Here ambiguity struggles with itself. It is not just that each moment of language can become ambiguous and say something different from what it is saying, but that the general meaning of language is unclear: we don't know if it is expressing or representing, if it is a thing or means that thing; if it is there to be forgotten or if it only makes us forget it so that we will see it; if it is transparent because what it says has so little meaning or clear because of the exactness with which it says it, obscure because it says too much, opaque because it says nothing. There is ambiguity everywhere: in its trivial exterior—but what is most frivolous may be the mask of the serious; in its disinterestedness—but behind this disinterestedness lie the forces of the world and it connives with them without knowing them, or again, ambiguity uses this disinterestedness to safeguard the absolute nature of the values without which action would stop or become mortal; its unreality is therefore both a principle of action and the incapacity to act: in the same way that the fiction in itself is truth and also indifference to truth; in the same way that if it allies itself with morality, it corrupts itself, and if it rejects morality, it still perverts itself; in the same way that it is nothing if it is not its own end, but it cannot have its end in itself, because it is without end, it ends outside itself, in history, etc.

All these reversals from *pro* to *contra*—and those described here—undoubtedly have very different causes. We have seen that literature assigns itself irreconcilable tasks. We have seen that in moving from the writer to the reader, from the labor to the finished work, it passes through contradictory moments and can only place itself in the affirmation of all the opposing moments. But all these contradictions, these hostile demands, these divisions and oppositions, so different in origin, kind, and meaning, refer back to an ultimate ambiguity whose strange effect is to attract literature to an unstable point where it can indiscriminately change both its meaning and its sign.

This ultimate vicissitude keeps the work in suspense in such a way that it can choose whether to take on a positive or a negative value and, as though it were pivoting invisibly around an invisible axis, enter the daylight of affirmations or the back-light of negations, without its style, genre, or subject being accountable for the radical transformation. Neither the content of the words nor their form is involved here. Whether the work is obscure or clear, poetry or prose, insignificant, important, whether it speaks of a pebble or of God, there is something in it that does not depend on its qualities and that deep within itself is always in the process of changing the work from the ground up. It is as though in the very heart of literature and language, beyond the visible movements that transform them, a point of instability were reserved, a power to work substantial metamorphoses, a power capable of changing everything about it without changing anything. This instability can appear to be the effect of a disintegrating force, since it can cause the strongest, most forceful work to become a work of unhappiness and ruin, but this disintegration is also a form of construction, if it suddenly causes distress to turn into hope and destruction into an element of the indestructible. How can such imminence of change, present in the depths of language quite apart from the meaning that affects it and the reality of that language, nevertheless be present in that meaning and in that reality? Could it be that the meaning of a word introduces something else into the word along with it, something which, although it protects the precise signification of the word and does not threaten that signification, is capable of completely modifying the meaning and modifying the material value of the word? Could there be a force at once friendly and hostile hidden in the intimacy of speech, a weapon intended to build and to destroy, which would act behind signification rather than upon signification? Do we have to suppose a meaning for the meaning of words that, while determining that meaning, also surrounds this determination with an ambiguous indeterminacy that wavers between yes and no?

But we can't suppose anything: we have questioned this meaning of the meaning of words at length, this meaning which is as much the movement of a word towards its truth as it is its return through the reality of language to the obscure depths of existence; we have questioned this absence by which the thing is annihilated, destroyed in order to become being and idea. It is *that life which supports death and maintains itself in it*—death, the amazing power of the negative, or freedom, through whose work existence is detached from itself and made significant. Now, nothing can prevent this power—at the very moment it is trying to understand things and, in language, to specify words—nothing can prevent it from continuing to assert itself as continually differing possibility, and nothing can stop it from perpetuating an irreducible *double meaning*, a choice whose terms are covered over with an ambiguity that makes them identical to one another even as it makes them opposite.

If we call this power negation or unreality or death, then presently death, negation, and unreality, at work in the depths of language, will signify the advent of truth in the world, the construction of intelligible being, the formation of meaning. But just as suddenly, the sign changes:

meaning no longer represents the marvel of comprehension, but instead refers us to the nothingness of death, and intelligible being signifies only the rejection of existence, and the absolute concern for truth is expressed by an incapacity to act in a real way. Or else death is perceived as a civilizing power which results in a comprehension of being. But at the same time, a death that results in being represents an absurd insanity, the curse of existence—which contains within itself both death and being and is neither being nor death. Death ends in being: this is man's hope and his task, because nothingness itself helps to make the world, nothingness is the creator of the world in man as he works and understands. Death ends in being: this is man's laceration, the source of his unhappy fate, since by man death comes to being and by man meaning rests on nothingness; the only way we can comprehend is by denying ourselves existence, by making death *possible*, by contaminating what we comprehend with the nothingness of death, so that if we emerge from being, we fall outside the possibility of death, and the way out becomes the disappearance of every way out.

This original double meaning, which lies deep inside every word like a condemnation that is still unknown and a happiness that is still invisible, is the source of literature, because literature is the form this double meaning has chosen in which to show itself behind the meaning and value of words, and the question it asks is the question asked by literature.

The Essential Solitude

It seems we have learned something about art when we experience what the word solitude designates. This word has been tossed around much too freely. Yet what does it mean to "be alone"? When is one alone? As we ask ourselves this question, we should not simply return to thoughts that we find moving. Solitude on the level of the world is a wound we do not need to comment on here.

Nor do we have in mind the solitude of the artist, the solitude which he is said to need if he is to practice his art. When Rilke writes to the Comtesse de Solms-Laubach (August 3, 1907): "Except for two short interruptions, I have not pronounced a single word for weeks; at last my solitude has closed in and I am in my work like a pit in its fruit," the solitude he speaks of is not essentially solitude: it is self-communion.

The solitude of the work.

In the solitude of the work—the work of art, the literary work— we see a more essential solitude. It excludes the self-satisfied isolation of individualism, it is unacquainted with the search for difference; it is not dissipated by the fact of sustaining a virile relationship in a task that covers the mastered extent of the day. The person who is writing the work is thrust to one side, the person who has written the work is dismissed. What is more, the person who is dismissed does not know it. This ignorance saves him, diverts him and allows him to go on. The writer never knows if the work is done. What he has finished in one book, he begins again or destroys in another. Valéry, who celebrates this privilege of the infinite in the work, still sees only its easiest aspect: the fact that the work is infinite means (to him) that although the artist is not capable of ending it, he is nevertheless capable of turning it into the enclosed space of an endless task whose incompleteness develops mastery of the spirit, expresses that mastery, expresses it by developing it in the form of power. At a certain point, circumstances—that is, history—in the form of an editor, financial demands, social duties, pronounce the missing end and the artist, freed by a purely compulsory outcome, pursues the incomplete elsewhere.

According to this point of view, the infinity of the work is simply the infinity of the spirit. The spirit tries to accomplish itself in a single work, instead of realizing itself in the infinity of works and the movement of history. But Valéry was in no way a hero. He chose to talk about everything, to write about everything: thus, the scattered whole of the world diverted him from the rigor of the unique whole of the work—he amiably allowed himself to be turned away from it. The *etc.* was hiding behind the diversity of thoughts, of subjects.

Nevertheless, the work—the work of art, the literary work—is neither finished nor unfinished: it is. What it says is exclusively that: that it is—and nothing more. Outside of that, it is nothing. Anyone who tries to make it express more finds nothing, finds that it expresses nothing. Anyone who lives in dependence on the work, whether because he is writing it or reading it, belongs to the solitude of something that expresses only the word *being*: a word that the language protects by hiding it or that the language causes to appear by disappearing into the silent void of the work.

The first framework of the solitude of the work is this absence of need which never permits it to be called finished or unfinished. The work can have no proof, just as it can have no use. It cannot be verified—truth can lay hold of it, renown illuminate it: this existence concerns it not at all, this obviousness makes it neither certain nor real, nor does it make it manifest.

The work is solitary: that does not mean that it remains incommunicable, that it lacks a reader. But the person who reads it enters into that affirmation of the solitude of the work, just as the one who writes it belongs to the risk of that solitude.

The work, the book.

If we want to examine more closely what such statements suggest, perhaps we should look for their source. The writer writes a book, but the book is not yet the work, the work is not a work until the word *being* is pronounced in it, in the violence of a beginning which is its own; this event occurs when the work is the innermost part of someone writing it and of someone reading it. We can therefore ask ourselves this: if solitude is the writer's risk, doesn't it express the fact that he is turned, oriented towards the open violence of the work, never grasping more than its substitute, its approach, and its illusion in the form of the book? The writer belongs to the work, but what belongs to him is only a book, a mute accumulation of sterile words, the most meaningless thing in the world. The writer who experiences this void simply believes that the work is unfinished, and he believes that with a little more effort and the luck of some favorable moments, he—and only he—will be able to finish it. And so he sets back to work. But what he wants to finish, by himself, remains something interminable, it ties him to an illusory labor. And in the end, the work ignores him, it closes on his absence, in the impersonal, anonymous statement that it is—and nothing more. Which we express by remarking that the artist, who only finishes his work at the moment he dies, never knows his work. And we may have to reverse that remark, because isn't the writer dead as soon as the work exists, as he himself sometimes forsees, when he experiences a very strange kind of worklessness.[1]

---

[1] This is not the situation of the man who works and accomplishes his task and whose task escapes him by transforming itself in the world. What this man makes is transformed, but in the world, and he recaptures it through the world, at least if he can recapture it, if alienation is not immobilized, if it is not diverted to the advantage of a few, but continues until the completion of the world. On the contrary, what the writer has in view is the work, and what he writes is a book. The book, as such, can become an active event in the world (an action, however, that is always reserved and insufficient), but it is not action the artist has in view, but the work, and what makes the book a substitute for the work is enough to make it a thing that, like the work, does not arise from the truth of the world; and it is an almost frivolous thing, if it has neither the reality of the work nor the seriousness of real labor in the world.

"Noli me legere."

The same situation can also be described this way: a writer never reads his work. For him, it is the unreadable, a secret, and he cannot remain face to face with it. A secret, because he is separated from it. Yet this impossibility of reading is not a purely negative movement, rather it is the only real approach the author can have to what we call a work. Where there is still only a book, the abrupt Noli me legere already causes the horizon of another power to appear. An experience that is fleeting, though immediate. It does not have the force of a prohibition, it is a statement that emerges from the play and the meaning of the words—the insistent, harsh and poignant statement that what is there, in the inclusive presence of a definitive text, still rejects—is the rude and caustic emptiness of rejection—or else excludes, with the authority of indifference, the person who has written it and now wants to recapture it by reading it. The impossibility of reading is the discovery that now, in the space opened by creation, there is no more room for creation—and no other possibility for the writer than to keep on writing the same work. No one who has written the work can live near it, dwell near it. This is the very decision that dismisses him, that cuts him off, that turns him into the survivor, the workless, unemployed, inert person on whom art does not depend.

The writer cannot dwell near the work: he can only write it, and once it is written he can only discern the approach to it in the abrupt Noli me legere that distances him, that moves him away or forces him to return to that "remove" where he first came in, to become the understanding of what he had to write. So that now he finds himself back again, in some sense at the beginning of his task, and he rediscovers the neighborhood of the outside, the errant intimacy of the outside, which he was not able to make into a dwelling.

Perhaps this ordeal points us in the direction of what we are looking for. The writer's solitude, then, this condition that is his risk, arises from the fact that in the work he belongs to what is always before the work. Through him the work arrives, is the firmness of a beginning, but he himself belongs to a time dominated by the indecision of beginning again. The obsession that ties him to a privileged theme, that makes him repeat what he has already said, sometimes with the power of enriched talent, but sometimes with the prolixity of an extraordinarily impoverishing repetition, less and less forcefully, more and more monotonously, illustrates his apparent need to come back to the same point, to retrace the same paths, to persevere and begin again what, for him, never really begins, to belong to the shadow of events instead of the object, to what allows the words themselves to become images, appearances—instead of signs, values, the power of truth.

Persecutive prehension.

It occurs that a man who is holding a pencil may want very much to let go of it, but his hand will not let go: quite the opposite— it tightens, it has no intention of opening. The other hand intervenes with more success, but then we see the hand that we may call sick slowly gesturing, trying to recapture the object that is moving away. What is strange is the slowness of this gesture. The hand moves through a time that is hardly human, that is neither the time of viable action nor the time of hope, but rather the shadow of time which is itself the shadow of a hand slipping in an unreal way towards an object that has become its shadow. At certain moments, this hand feels a very great need to grasp: it must take the pencil, this is necessary, this is an order, an imperious requirement. The phenomenon is known as "persecutive prehension."

The writer seems to be master of his pen, he can become capable of great mastery over words, over what he wants to make them express. But this mastery only manages to put him in contact, keep him in contact, with a fundamental passivity in which the word, no longer anything beyond its own appearance, the shadow of a word, can never be mastered or even grasped; it remains impossible to grasp, impossible to relinquish, the unsettled moment of fascination.

The writer's mastery does not lie in the hand that writes, the "sick" hand that never lets go of the pencil, that cannot let it go because it does not really hold what it is holding; what it holds belongs to shadow, and the hand itself is a shadow. Mastery is always the achievement of the other hand, the one that does not write, the one that can intervene just when it has to, grasp the pencil and take it away. Mastery, then, consists of the power to stop writing, to interrupt what is being written, giving its rights and its exclusive cutting edge back to the instant.

We must resume our questions. We have said: the writer belongs to the work, but what belongs to him—what he finishes alone—is only a book. The restriction of "only" responds to the expression "alone." The writer never stands before the work, and where there is a work, he does not know it, or more exactly, he is ignorant of his very ignorance, it is only present in the impossibility of reading, an ambiguous experience that sends him back to work.

The writer sets back to work. Why doesn't he stop writing? If he breaks with the work, as Rimbaud did, why does that break strike us as a mysterious impossibility? Is it simply that he wants a perfect work, and if he keeps on working at it, is this only because the perfection is never perfect enough? Does he even write for the sake of a work? Is he preoccupied by it as the thing that will put an end to his task, as a goal worthy of all his efforts? Not at all. And the work is never that for the sake of which one is able to write (that for the sake of which one might relate to what is written as to the exercise of a power).

The fact that the writer's task comes to an end when he dies is what hides the fact that because of this task his life slips into the unhappiness of infinity.

The interminable, the incessant.

The solitude that comes to the writer through the work of literature is revealed by this: the act of writing is now interminable, incessant. The writer no longer belongs to the authoritative realm where expressing oneself means expressing the exactness and certainty of things and of values depending on the meaning of their limits. What is written consigns the person who must write to a statement over which he has no authority, a statement that is itself without consistency, that states nothing, that is not the repose, the dignity of silence, because it is what is still speaking when everything has been said, what does not precede speech because it instead prevents it from being a beginning of speech, just as it withdraws from speech the right and the power to interrupt itself. To write is to break the bond uniting the speech to myself, to break the relationship that makes me talk towards "you" and gives me speech within the understanding that this speech receives from you, because it addresses you, it is the address that begins in me because it ends in you. To write is to break this link. What is more, it withdraws language from the course of the world, it deprives it of what makes it a power such that when I speak, it is the world that is spoken, it is the day that is built by work, action and time.

The act of writing is interminable, incessant. The writer, they say, stops saying "I." Kafka observes with surprise, with enchantment and delight, that as soon as he was able to substitute "he" for "I" he entered literature. This is true, but the transformation is much more profound. The writer belongs to a language no one speaks, a language that is not addressed to anyone, that has no center, that reveals nothing. He can believe he is asserting himself in this language, but what he is asserting is completely without a self. To the extent that, as a writer, he accedes to what is written, he can never again express himself and he cannot appeal to you either, nor yet let anyone else speak. Where he is, only being speaks, which means that speech no longer speaks, but simply is— dedicates itself to the pure passivity of being.

When to write means to consign oneself to the interminable, the writer who agrees to sustain its essence loses the power to say "I." He then loses the power to make others say "I." Thus it is impossible for him to give life to characters whose freedom would be guaranteed by his creative force. The idea of a character, like the traditional form of the novel, is only one of the compromises that a writer—drawn out of himself by literature in search of its essence—uses to try to save his relations with the world and with himself.

To write is to make oneself the echo of what cannot stop talking— and because of this, in order to become its echo, I must to a certain extent impose silence on it. To this incessant speech I bring the decisiveness, the authority of my own silence. Through my silent mediation, I make perceptible the uninterrupted affirmation, the giant murmur in which language, by opening, becomes image, becomes imaginary, an eloquent depth, an indistinct fullness that is empty. The source of this silence is the self-effacement to which the person who writes is invited. Or, this silence is the resource of his mastery, the right to intervene maintained by the hand that does not write— the part of himself that can always say no, and, when necessary, appeals to time, restores the future.

When we admire the tone of a work, responding to the tone as what is most authentic about it, what are we referring to? Not the style, and not the interest and the quality of the language, but precisely the silence, the virile force through which the person who writes, having deprived himself of himself, having renounced himself, has nevertheless maintained within his effacement the authority of a power, the decision to be silent, so that in this silence what speaks without beginning or end can take on form, coherence and meaning.

Tone is not the voice of the writer, but the intimacy of the silence he imposes on speech, which makes this silence still *his own*, what remains of himself in the discretion that sets him to one side. Tone makes the great writers, but perhaps the work is not concerned about what makes them great.

In the effacement to which he is invited, the "great writer" still restrains himself: what speaks is no longer himself, but it is not the pure slipping of the speech of no one. Of the effaced "I," it retains the authoritarian, though silent affirmation. It retains the cutting edge, the violent rapidity of active time, of the instant. This is how he is preserved inside the work, is contained where there is no more restraint. But because of this the work, too, retains a content; it is not completely interior to itself.

The writer we call classic—at least in France—sacrifices the speech that is his own within him, but in order to give voice to the universal. The calm of a form governed by rules, the certainty of a speech freed from caprice, in which impersonal generality speaks, assures him a relationship with truth. Truth that is beyond person and would like to be beyond time. Literature then has the glorious solitude of reason, that rarified life at the heart of the whole that would require resolution and courage—if that reason were not in fact the equilibrium of an orderly aristocratic society, that is, the noble contentment of a section of society that concentrates the whole in itself, by isolating itself and maintaining itself above what permits it to live.

When to write is to discover the interminable, the writer who enters this region does not go beyond himself towards the universal. He does not go towards a world that is more sure, more beautiful, better justified, where everything is arranged in the light of a just day. He does not discover the beautiful language that speaks honorably for everyone. What speaks in him is the fact that in one way or another he is no longer himself, he is already no longer anyone. The "he" that is substituted for "I"—this is the solitude that comes to the writer through the work. "He" does not indicate objective disinterest, creative detachment. "He" does not glorify the consciousness of someone other than me, the soaring of a human life that, within the imaginary space of the work of art, keeps its freedom to say "I." "He" is myself having become no one, someone else having become the other; it is the fact that there, where I am, I can no longer address myself to myself, and that the person who addresses himself to me does not say "I," is not himself.

Recourse to the "Journal."

It is perhaps striking that the moment the work becomes the pursuit of art, becomes literature, the writer feels a growing need to preserve a relationship with himself. He feels an extreme reluctance to relinquish himself in favor of that neutral power, formless, without a destiny, which lies behind everything that is written, and his reluctance and apprehension are revealed by the concern, common to so many authors, to keep what he calls his *Journal*. This is quite unlike the so-called romantic complacencies. The Journal is not essentially a confession, a story about oneself. It is a Memorial. What does the writer have to remember? Himself, who he is when he is not writing, when he is living his daily life, when he is alive and real, and not dying and without truth. But the strange thing is that the means he uses to recall himself to himself is the very element of forgetfulness: the act of writing. Yet this is why the truth of the Journal does not lie in the interesting and literary remarks to be found in it, but in the insignificant details that tie it to everyday reality. The Journal represents the series of reference points that a writer establishes as a way of recognizing himself, when he anticipates the dangerous metamorphosis he is vulnerable to. It is a path that is still viable, a sort of parapet walk that runs alongside the other path, overlooks it and sometimes coincides with it, the other being the one where the endless task is wandering. Here, real things are still spoken of. Here, the one who speaks retains his name and speaks in his name, and the date inscribed belongs to a common time in which what happens really happens. The Journal—this book that is apparently completely solitary—is often written out of fear and dread in the face of the solitude that comes to the writer through the work.

Recourse to the Journal indicates that the person writing does not want to break with the happiness, the decorum of days that are really days and that really follow one another. The Journal roots the movement of writing in time, in the humbleness of the everyday, dated and preserved by its date. Perhaps what is written there is already only insincerity, perhaps it is said without concern for what is true, but it is said under the safeguard of the event, it belongs to the affairs, the incidents, the commerce of the world, to an active present, to a stretch of time that is perhaps completely worthless and insignificant, but that at least cannot turn back; it is the work of something that goes beyond itself, goes towards the future, goes there definitively.

The Journal shows that already the person writing is no longer capable of belonging to time through ordinary firmness of action, through the community created by work, by profession, through the simplicity of intimate speech, the force of thoughtlessness. Already he does not really belong to history anymore, but he does not want to lose time either, and since he no longer knows how to do anything but write, at least he writes at the demand of his day-to-day story and in keeping with his everyday preoccupations. Often writers who keep journals are the most literary of all writers, but perhaps this is precisely because in doing so they avoid the extreme of literature, if literature is in fact the fascinating domain of the absence of time.

The fascination of the absence of time.

To write is to surrender oneself to the fascination of the absence of time. Here we are undoubtedly approaching the essence of solitude. The absence of time is not a purely negative mode. It is the time in which nothing begins, in which initiative is not possible, where before the affirmation there is already the recurrence of the affirmation. Rather than a purely negative mode, it is a time without negation, without decision, when *here* is also *nowhere*, when each thing withdraws into its image and the "I" that we are recognizes itself as it sinks into the neutrality of a faceless "he." The time of the absence of time is without a present, without a presence. This "without a present," however, does not refer to a past. *Formerly* had the dignity and the active force of *now*; memory still bears witness to this active force, memory which frees me from what would otherwise recall me, frees me from it by giving me the means to summon it freely, to dispose of it according to my present intention. Memory is the freedom from the past. But what is without a present does not accept the present of a memory either. Memory says of an event: that was, once, and now never again. The irremediable nature of what is without a present, of what is not even there as having been, says: that has never occurred, never a single first time, and yet it is resuming, again, again, infinitely. It is without end, without beginning. It is without a future.

The time of the absence of time is not dialectical. What appears in it is the fact that nothing appears, the being that lies deep within the absence of being, the being that is when there is nothing, that is no longer when there is something—as though there were beings only through the loss of being, when being is lacking. The reversal that constantly refers us back, in the absence of time, to the presence of absence, but to this presence as absence, to absence as affirmation of itself, affirmation in which nothing is affirmed, in which nothing ceases to be affirmed, in the aggravation of the indefinite—this movement is not dialectical. Contradictions do not exclude one another there, nor are they reconciled there; only time, for which negation becomes our power, can be the "unity of incompatible things." In the absence of time, what is new does not renew anything; what is present is not contemporary; what is present presents nothing, represents itself, belongs now and henceforth and at all times to recurrence. This is not, but comes back, comes as already and always past, so that I do not know it, but I recognize it, and this recognition destroys the power in me to know, the right to grasp, makes what cannot be grasped into something that cannot be relinquished, the inaccessible that I cannot cease attaining, what I cannot take but can only take back—and never give up.

This time is not the ideal immobility that is glorified under the name of the eternal. In the region we are trying to approach, here is submerged in nowhere, but nowhere is nevertheless here, and dead time is a real time in which death is present, in which it arrives but does not stop arriving, as though by arriving it rendered sterile the time that permits it to arrive. The dead present is the impossibility of realizing a presence—an impossibility that is present, that is there as that which doubles every present, the shadow of the present, which the present carries and hides in itself. When I am alone, in this present, I am not alone, but am already returning to myself in the form of Someone. Someone is there, where I am alone. The fact of being alone is that I belong to this dead time that is not my time, nor yours, nor common time, but the time of Someone. Someone is what is still present when no one is there. In the place where I am alone, I am not there, there is no one there, but the impersonal is there: the outside as what anticipates, precedes, dissolves all possibility of personal relationship. Someone is the faceless He, the One of which one is a part, but who is a part of it? No one is part of the One. "One" belongs to a region that cannot be brought into the light—not because it conceals a secret alien to all revelation, not even because it is radically dark, but because it transforms everything that has access to it, even light, into anonymous, impersonal being, the Not-true, the Not-real and yet always there. In this sense, the "One" is what appears closest to one when one dies.[2]

Where I am alone, day is no longer anything but the loss of an abode, it is an intimacy with the outside, the outside that is placeless and without repose. The act of coming here causes the one who comes to be part of the dispersal, the fissure in which the exterior is a stifling intrusion, the nakedness and cold of that in which one remains exposed, where space is the dizziness of being spaced. Then fascination reigns.

---

[2] When I am alone, I am not the one who is here and you are not the one I am far away from, nor other people, nor the world. At this point we begin to ponder the idea of "essential solitude and solitude in the world." [See Blanchot's four pages entitled "La solitude essentielle et la solitude dans le monde" in the appendix to L'Espace litteraire (Gallimard, 1955)—Tr.]

The image.

Why fascination? Seeing implies distance, the decision that causes separation, the power not to be in contact and to avoid the confusion of contact. Seeing means that this separation has nevertheless become an encounter. But what happens when what you see, even though from a distance, seems to touch you with a grasping contact, when the manner of seeing is a sort of touch, when seeing is a *contact* at a distance? What happens when what is seen imposes itself on your gaze, as though the gaze had been seized, touched, put in contact with appearance? Not an active contact, not the initiative and action that might still remain in a true touch; rather, the gaze is drawn, absorbed into an immobile movement and a depth without depth. What is given to us by contact at a distance is the image, and fascination is passion for the image.

What fascinates us, takes away our power to give it a meaning, abandons its "perceptible" nature, abandons the world, withdraws to the near side of the world and attracts us there, no longer reveals itself to us and yet asserts itself in a presence alien to the present in time and to presence in space. The split, which had been the possibility of seeing, solidifies, right inside the gaze, into impossibility. In this way, in the very thing that makes it possible, the gaze finds the power that neutralizes it—that does not suspend it or arrest it, but on the contrary prevents it from ever finishing, cuts it off from all beginning, makes it into a neutral, wandering glimmer that is not extinguished, that does not illuminate: the circle of the gaze, closed on itself. Here we have an immediate expression of the inversion that is the essence of solitude. Fascination is the gaze of solitude, the gaze of what is incessant and interminable, in which blindness is still vision, vision that is no longer the possibility of seeing, but the impossibility of not seeing, impossibility that turns into seeing, that perseveres—always and always—in a vision that does not end: a dead gaze, a gaze that has become the ghost of an eternal vision.

It can be said that a person who is fascinated does not perceive any real object, any real form, because what he sees does not belong to the world of reality, but to the indeterminate realm of fascination. A realm that is so to speak absolute. Distance is not excluded from it, but it is excessive, being the unlimited depth that lies behind the image, a depth that is not alive, not tractable, absolutely present though not provided, where objects sink when they become separated from their meaning, when they subside into their image. This realm of fascination, where what we see seizes our vision and makes it interminable, where our gaze solidifies into light, where light is the absolute sheen of an eye that we do not see, that we nevertheless do not leave off seeing because it is the mirror image of our own gaze, this realm is supremely attractive, fascinating: light that is also the abyss, horrifying and alluring, light in which we sink.

Our childhood fascinates us because it is the moment of fascination, it is fascinated itself, and this golden age seems bathed in a light that is splendid because it is unrevealed, but the fact is that this light is alien to revelation, has nothing to reveal, is pure reflection, a ray that is still only the radiance of an image. Perhaps the power of the maternal figure derives its brilliance from the very power of fascination, and one could say that if the Mother exerts this fascinating attraction, it is because she appears when the child lives completely under the gaze of fascination, and so concentrates in herself all the powers of enchantment. It is because the child is fascinated that the mother is fascinating, and this is also why all the impressions of our earliest years have a fixed quality that arises from fascination.

When someone who is fascinated sees something, he does not see it, properly speaking, but it touches him in his immediate proximity, it seizes him and monopolizes him, even though it leaves him absolutely at a distance. Fascination is tied in a fundamental way to the neutral, impersonal presence, the indeterminate One, the immense and faceless Someone. It is the relationship—one that is itself neutral and impersonal—that the gaze maintains with the depths that have no gaze and no contour, the absence that one sees because it is blinding.

The act of writing.

To write is to enter into the affirmation of solitude where fascination threatens. It is to yield to the risk of the absence of time, where eternal recommencement holds sway. It is to pass from the I to the He, so that what happens to me happens to no one, is anonymous because of the fact that it is my business, repeats itself in an infinite dispersal. To write is to arrange language under fascination and, through language, in language, remain in contact with the absolute milieu, where the thing becomes an image again, where the image, which had been allusion to a figure, becomes an allusion to what is without figure, and having been a form sketched on absence, becomes the unformed presence of that absence, the opaque and empty opening on what is when there is no more world, when there is no world yet.

Why this? Why should the act of writing have anything to do with this essential solitude, the essence of which is that in it, concealment appears?[3]

---

[3] We will not try to answer this question directly here. We will simply ask: just as a statue glorifies marble—and if all art tries to draw out into the daylight the elemental depths that the world denies and drives back as it asserts itself—isn't language in the poem, in literature, related to ordinary language in the same way that the image is related to the thing? We are apt to think that poetry is a language which, more than any other, does justice to images. Probably this is an allusion to a much more essential transformation: the poem is not a poem because it includes a certain number of figures, metaphors, comparisons. On the contrary, what is special about a poem is that nothing in it strikes a vivid image. We must therefore express what we are looking for in another way: in literature, doesn't language itself become entirely image, not a language containing images or putting reality into figures, but its own image, the image of language—and not a language full of imagery—or an imaginary language, a language no one speaks—that is to say, spoken from its own absence—in the same way that the image appears on the absence of the thing, a language that is also addressed to the shadow of events, not to their reality, because of the fact that the words that express them are not signs, but images, images of words and words in which things become images?

What are we trying to describe by saying this? Aren't we headed in a direction that will force us to return to opinions we were happy to relinquish, opinions similar to the old idea that art was an imitation, a copy of the real? If the language in a poem becomes its own image, doesn't that mean that poetic speech is always second, secondary? According to the customary analysis, an image exists after an object: it follows from it; we see, then we imagine. After the object comes the image. "After" seems to indicate a subordinate relationship. We speak in a real way, then we speak in an imaginary way, or we imagine ourselves speaking. Isn't poetic speech nothing more than a tracing, a weakened shadow, the transposition of the unique speaking language into a space where the requirements for effectiveness are attenuated? But perhaps the customary analysis is wrong. Perhaps, before we go any further, we should ask ourselves: but what is the image? (See the essay entitled "The Two Versions of the Imaginary.")

Two Versions of the Imaginary

But what is the image? When there is nothing, that is where the image finds its condition, but disappears into it. The image requires the neutrality and the effacement of the world, it wants everything to return to the indifferent depth where nothing is affirmed, it inclines towards the intimacy of what still continues to exist in the void; its truth lies there. But this truth exceeds it; what makes it possible is the limit where it ceases. Hence its dramatic aspect, the ambiguity it evinces, and the brilliant lie with which it is reproached. A superb power, says Pascal, which makes eternity into nothingness and nothingness into an eternity.

The image speaks to us, and it seems to speak intimately to us about ourselves. But intimately is to say too little; intimately then designates that level where the intimacy of the person breaks off, and in that motion points to the menacing nearness of a vague and empty outside that is the sordid background against which the image continues to affirm things in their disappearance. In this way, in connection with each thing, it speaks to us of less than the thing, but of us, and in connection with us, of less than us, of that less than nothing which remains when there is nothing.

The fortunate thing about the image is that it is a limit next to the indefinite. A thin ring, but one which does not keep us at such a remove from things that it saves us from the blind pressure of that remove. Through it, that remove is available to us. Through what there is of inflexibility in a reflection, we believe ourselves to be masters of the absence that has become an interval, and the dense void itself seems to open to the radiation of another day.

In this way the image fills one of its functions, which is to pacify, to humanize the unformed nothingness pushed towards us by the residue of being that cannot be eliminated. It cleans it up, appropriates it, makes it pleasant and pure and allows us to believe, in the heart of the happy dream which art too often permits, that at a distance from the real, and immediately behind it, we are finding, as a pure happiness and a superb satisfaction, the transparent eternity of the unreal.

"For," says Hamlet, "in that sleep of death what dreams may come, when we have shuffl'd off this mortal coil . . . " The image, present behind each thing and in some sense the dissolution of that thing and its continuance in its dissolution, also has, behind it, that heavy sleep of death in which dreams might come to us. When it wakes or when we wake it, it can very well represent an object to us in a luminous *formal* halo; it has sided with the *depth*, with elemental materiality, the still undetermined absence of form (the world that oscillates between the adjective and the substantive), before sinking into the unformed prolixity of indetermination. This is the reason for its characteristic passivity: a passivity that makes us submit to it, even when we are summoning it, and causes its fleeting transparency to arise from the obscurity of destiny returned to its essence, which is that of a shadow.

But when we confront things themselves, if we stare at a face, a corner of a room, doesn't it also sometimes happen that we abandon ourselves to what we see, that we are at its mercy, powerless before this presence that is suddenly strangely mute and passive? This is true, but what has happened is that the thing we are staring at has sunk into its image, that the image has returned to that depth of impotence into which everything falls back. The "real" is that with which our relationship is always alive and which always leaves us the initiative, addressing that power we have to begin, that free communication with the beginning that is ourselves; and to the extent that we are in the day, the day is still contemporary with its awakening.

According to the usual analysis, the image exists after the object: the image follows from it; we see, then we imagine. After the object comes the image. "After" means that first the thing must move away in order to allow itself to be grasped again. But that distancing is not the simple change of place of a moving object, which nevertheless remains the same. Here the distancing is at the heart of the thing. The thing was there, we grasped it in the living motion of a comprehensive action— and once it has become an image it instantly becomes ungraspable, noncontemporary, impassive, not the same thing distanced, but that thing as distancing, the present thing in its absence, the thing graspable because ungraspable, appearing as something that has disappeared, the return of what does not come back, the strange heart of the distance as the life and unique heart of the thing.

In the image, the object again touches something it had mastered in order to be an object, something against which it had built and defined itself, but now that its value, its signification, is suspended, now that the world is abandoning it to worklessness and putting it to one side, the truth in it withdraws, the elemental claims it, which is the impoverishment, the enrichment that consecrates it as image.

Nevertheless: doesn't the reflection always seem more spiritual than the object reflected? Isn't it the ideal expression of that object, its presence freed of existence, its form without matter? And artists who exile themselves in the illusion of images, isn't their task to idealize beings, to elevate them to their disembodied resemblance?

The image, the mortal remains.

At first sight, the image does not resemble a cadaver, but it could be that the strangeness of a cadaver is also the strangeness of the image. What we call the mortal remains evades the usual categories: something is there before us that is neither the living person himself nor any sort of reality, neither the same as the one who was alive, nor another, nor another thing. What is there, in the absolute calm of what has found its place, nevertheless does not realize the truth of being fully here. Death suspends relations with the place, even though the dead person relies heavily on it as the only base left to him. Yes, the fact is that that base is lacking, place is missing, the cadaver is not in its place. Where is it? It is not here and yet it is not elsewhere; nowhere? but the fact is that then nowhere is here. The cadaverous presence establishes a relation between here and nowhere. First of all, in the mortuary chamber and on the death bed, the repose that must be maintained shows how fragile the ultimate position is. Here is the cadaver, but here, in turn, becomes a cadaver: "here below," speaking absolutely, with no "up there" exalting itself any longer. The place where one dies is not just any place at all. One does not willingly transport these remains from one spot to another:

death jealously secures its place and unites with it to the very bottom, in such a way that the indifference of that place, the fact that it is nevertheless just any place at all, becomes the depth of its presence as death, becomes the support of indifference, the yawning intimacy of a nowhere without difference, yet one that must be situated here.

Remaining is not accessible to the one who dies. The deceased, we say, is no longer of this world, he has left it behind him, but what is left behind is precisely this cadaver, which is not of this world either—even though it is here—which is, rather, behind the world, something the living person (and not the deceased) has left behind him and which now affirms, on the basis of this, the possibility of a world-behind, a return backwards, an indefinite survival, indeterminate, indifferent, about which we only know that human reality, when it comes to an end, reconstitutes its presence and proximity. This is an impression we can call common: someone who has just died is first of all very close to the condition of a thing—a familiar thing that we handle and approach, that does not keep us at a distance and whose soft passivity reveals only its sad impotence. Of course dying is a unique event, and someone who dies "in your arms" is in some sense your fellow creature forever, but he is dead, now. Everyone knows that action must be taken quickly, not so much because the stiffness of the cadaver will make it more difficult, but because human action will very soon be "displaced." Very soon there will be—undisplaceable, untouchable, riveted to here by the strangest kind of embrace and yet drifting with it, dragging it farther below— no longer an inanimate object but Someone, the insupportable image and the figure of the unique becoming anything at all.

The resemblance of cadavers.

The striking thing, when this moment comes, is that though the remains appear in the strangeness of their solitude, as something disdainfully withdrawn from us, just when the sense of an interhuman relationship is broken, when our mourning, our care and the prerogative of our former passions, no longer able to know their object, fall back on us, come back towards us—at this moment, when the presence of the cadaver before us is the presence of the unknown, it is also now that the lamented dead person begins to *resemble himself*.

Himself: isn't that an incorrect expression? Shouldn't we say: the person he was, when he was alive? Himself is nevertheless the right word. Himself designates the impersonal, distant and inaccessible being that resemblance, in order to be able to be resemblance to someone, also draws towards the day. Yes, it is really he, the dear living one; but all the same it is more than him, he is more beautiful, more imposing, already monumental and so absolutely himself that he is in some sense *doubled* by himself, united to the solemn impersonality of himself by resemblance and by image. This large-scale being, important and superb, who impresses the living as the apparition of the original—until then unknown—sentence of the last Judgment inscribed in the depths of the being and triumphantly expressing itself with the help of the distance: he may recall, because of his sovereign appearance, the great images of classic art. If this connection is valid, the question of the idealism of this art will seem rather vain; and the fact that in the end idealism should have no guarantee but a cadaver—this can be retained in order to show how much the apparent spirituality, the pure formal virginity of the image is fundamentally linked to the elemental strangeness and to the shapeless heaviness of the being that is present in absence.

If we look at him again, this splendid being who radiates beauty: he is, I can see, perfectly like himself; he resembles *himself*. The cadaver is its own image. He no longer has any relations with this world, in which he still appears, except those of an image, an obscure possibility, a shadow which is constantly present behind the living form and which now, far from separating itself from that form, completely transforms itself into a shadow. The cadaver is reflection making itself master of the reflected life, absorbing it, substantially identifying itself with it by making it lose its value in terms of use and truth and change into something incredible—unusual and neutral. And if the cadaver resembles to such a degree, that is because it is, at a certain moment, preeminently resemblance, and it is also nothing more. It is the equal, equal to an absolute, overwhelming and marvelous degree. But what does it resemble? Nothing.

This is why each living man, really, does not yet have any resemblance. Each man, in the rare moments when he shows a similar to himself, seems to be only more distant, close to a dangerous neutral region, *astray* in *himself,* and in some sense his own ghost, already having no other life than that of the return.

By analogy, we can also recall that a utensil, once it has been damaged, becomes its own *image* (and sometimes an esthetic object: "those outmoded, fragmented, unusable, almost incomprehensible, perverse objects" that André Breton loved). In this case, the utensil, no longer disappearing in its use, *appears.* This appearance of the object is that of resemblance and reflection: one might say it is its double. The category of art is linked to this possibility objects have of "appearing," that is, of abandoning themselves to pure and simple resemblance behind which there is nothing—except being. Only what has surrendered itself to the image appears, and everything that appears is, in this sense, imaginary.

The resemblance of cadavers is a haunting obsession, but the act of haunting is not the unreal visitation of the ideal: what haunts is the inaccessible which one cannot rid oneself of, what one does not find and what, because of that, does not allow one to avoid it. The ungraspable is what one does not escape. The fixed image is without repose, especially in the sense that it does not pose anything, does not establish anything. Its fixity, like that of the mortal remains, is the position of that which remains because it lacks a place (the fixed idea is not a point of departure, a position from which one could move away and progress, it is not a beginning, but a beginning again). We know that in spite of its so tranquil and firm immobility the cadaver we have dressed, have brought as close as possible to a normal appearance by obliterating the disgrace of its illness, is not resting. The spot it occupies is dragged along by it, sinks with it, and in this dissolution assails—even for us, the others who remain—the possibility of a sojourn. We know that at "a certain moment," the power of death causes it to leave the fine place that has been assigned to it. Even though the cadaver is tranquilly lying in state on its bier, it is also everywhere in the room, in the house. At any moment, it can be elsewhere than where it is, where we are without it, where there is nothing, an invading presence, an obscure and vain fullness. The belief that at a certain moment the dead person begins to wander, must be ascribed to the intuition of that *error* he now represents.

Finally, an end must be put to what is endless: one does not live with dead people under penalty of seeing *here* sink into an unfathomable *nowhere*, a fall that is illustrated by the fall of the House of Usher. The dear departed, then, is conveyed to another place, and undoubtedly the site is only symbolically at a distance, in no way unlocatable, but it is nevertheless true that the *here* of *here lies*, full of names, of solid constructions, or affirmations of identity, is preeminently the anonymous and impersonal place, as though, within the limits drawn for it and in the vain guise of a pretension capable of surviving everything, the monotony of an infinite erosion were at work obliterating the living truth that characterizes every place, and making it equal to the absolute neutrality of death.

(This slow disappearance, this infinite attrition of the end, may illuminate the very remarkable passion of certain women who become poisoners: their pleasure does not lie in causing suffering nor even in killing slowly, bit by bit, or by stifling, but rather it lies in reaching the indefiniteness that is death by poisoning time, by transforming it into an imperceptible consumption; in this way they brush with horror, they live furtively below all life, in a pure decomposition which nothing divulges, and the poison is the white substance of that eternity. Feuerbach tells of one poisoner for whom poison was a lover, a companion to whom she felt passionately drawn; when, after she had been in prison for several months, she was presented with a small bag of arsenic that belonged to her and was asked to identify it, she trembled with joy, she experienced a moment of ecstasy.)

The image and signification.

Man is made in his own image: this is what we learn from the strangeness of the resemblance of cadavers. But this formula should first of all be understood this way: *man is unmade according to his image.* The image has nothing to do with signification, meaning, as implied by the existence of the world, the effort of truth, the law and the brightness of the day. Not only is the *image* of an object not the *meaning* of that object and of no help in comprehending it, but it tends to withdraw it from its meaning by maintaining it in the immobility of a resemblance that has nothing to resemble.

Certainly we can always recapture the image and make it serve the truth of the world; but then we would be reversing the relationship that characterizes it: in this case, the image becomes the follower of the object, what comes after it, what remains of it and allows us to have it still available to us when nothing is left of it, a great resource, a fecund and judicious power. Practical life and the accomplishment of real tasks demand this reversal. Classical art, at least in theory, implied it too, glorying in bringing back resemblance to a figure and the image to a body, in reincorporating it: the image became vitalizing negation, the ideal labor through which man, capable of denying nature, raised it to a higher meaning, either in order to know it, or to take pleasure in it through admiration. In this way, art was both ideal and true, faithful to the figure and faithful to the truth that is without figure. Impersonality, in the end, verified the works. But impersonality was also the troubling site of encounter where the noble ideal, concerned for values, and the anonymous, blind and impersonal resemblance exchanged places and passed for each other in a mutual deception. "How vain is painting, that excites admiration through its resemblance to things whose originals one does not admire at all!" Nothing more striking, then, than this strong distrust of Pascal's for resemblance, as he felt that it surrendered things to the sovereignty of the void and to the most vain kind of persistence, an eternity which, as he said, is nothingness, nothingness which is eternity.

The two versions.

Thus there are two possibilites for the image, two versions of the imaginary, and this duplicity comes from the initial double meaning produced by the power of the negative and the fact that death is sometimes the work of truth in the world, sometimes the perpetuity of something that does not tolerate either a beginning or an end.

It is therefore really true that in man, as contemporary philosophies have it, comprehension and knowledge are connected to what we call finitude, but where is the end in this finitude? It is certainly contained in the possibility that is death, but it is also "taken up again" by it, if in death the possibility that is death dissolves too. And it still seems, even though all of human history signifies the hope of overcoming that ambiguity, that to settle it or to go beyond it always involves in one sense or in the other the greatest dangers: as though the choice between death as possibility of comprehension and death as horror of the impossibility also had to be the choice between sterile truth and the prolixity of the not-true, as though scarcity were tied to comprehension and fecundity to horror. This is why ambiguity, though it alone makes choice possible, always remains present in choice itself.

But in this case, how does *ambiguity* manifest itself? What is happening, for example, when one sees an event as image?

To experience an event as image is not to free oneself of that event, to dissociate oneself from it, as is asserted by the esthetic version of the image and the serene ideal of classical art, but neither is it to engage oneself with it through a free decision: it is to let oneself be taken by it, to go from the region of the real, where we hold ourselves at a distance from things the better to use them, to that other region where distance holds us, this distance which is now unliving, unavailable depth, an inappreciable remoteness become in some sense the sovereign and last power of things. This movement implies infinite degrees. Thus psychoanalysis says that the image, far from leaving us outside of things and making us live in the mode of gratuitous fantasy, seems to surrender us profoundly to ourselves. The image is intimate, because it makes our intimacy an exterior power that we passively submit to: outside of us, in the backward motion of the world that the image provokes, the depth of our passion trails along, astray and brilliant.

Magic takes its power from this transformation. Through a methodical technique, it induces things to awaken as reflection, and consciousness to thicken into a thing. From the moment we are outside ourselves—in that ecstasy that which is the image—the "real" enters an equivocal realm where there is no longer any limit, nor any interval, nor moments, and where each thing, absorbed in the void of its reflection, draws near the consciousness, which has allowed itself to be filled up by an anonymous fullness. Thus the universal unity seems recreated. Thus, behind things, the soul of each thing obeys the spells now possessed by the ecstatic man who has abandoned himself to the "universe." The paradox of magic is certainly obvious: it claims to be initiative and free domination, whereas in order to create itself, it accepts the reign of passivity, that reign in which there are no ends. But its intention remains instructive: what it wants is to act on the world (manoeuver it), beginning with being which precedes the world, the eternal this-side where action is impossible. This is why it would rather turn towards the strangeness of the cadaver, and its only serious name is black magic.

To experience an event as image is not to have an image of that event, nor is it to give it the gratuitousness of the imaginary. The event, in this case, really takes place, and yet does it "really" take place? What happens seizes us, as the image would seize us, that is, it deprives us, of it and of ourselves, keeps us outside, makes this outside a presence where "I" does not recognize "itself." A movement that involves infinite degrees. What we have called the two versions of the imaginary, this fact that the image can certainly help us to recapture the thing in an ideal way, being, then, its vitalizing negation, but also, on the level we are drawn to by its own weight, constantly threatening to send us back, no longer to the absent thing, but to absence as presence, to the neutral double of the object, in which belonging to the world has vanished: this duplicity is not such that one can pacify it with an "either, or else," capable of permitting a choice and of taking away from choice the ambiguity that makes it possible. This duplicity itself refers to a double meaning that is ever more primary.

The levels of ambiguity.

If thought could, for a moment, maintain ambiguity, it would be tempted to say that there are three levels on which it occurs. On the level of the world, ambiguity is the possibility of understanding; meaning always escapes into another meaning; misunderstanding is useful to comprehension, it expresses the truth of the understanding that one is never understood once and for all.

Another level is that expressed by the two versions of the imaginary. Here, there is no longer a question of a perpetual double meaning, of the misunderstanding that helps or deceives understanding. Here, what speaks in the name of the image "sometimes" still speaks of the world, "sometimes" introduces us into the indeterminate region of fascination, "sometimes" gives us the power to use things in their absence and through fiction, thus keeping us within a horizon rich in meaning, "sometimes" makes us slip into the place where things are perhaps present, but in their image, and where the image is the moment of passivity, having no value either significative or affective, being the passion of indifference. Nevertheless, what we distinguish by saying "sometimes, sometimes" ambiguity says by saying always, to a certain extent, the one and the other; it expresses, moreover, the significant image in the heart of fascination, but already fascinates us through the clarity of the most pure, the most formed image. Here, *meaning* does not escape into another meaning, but into the *other* of all meaning and, because of ambiguity, nothing has meaning, but everything *seems* to have infinitely much meaning: meaning is no longer anything more than a semblance; the semblance causes the meaning to become infinitely rich, causes this infinitude of meaning to have no need of being developed, to be immediate, that is, also to be incapable of being developed, to be simply immediately empty.[1]

---

[1] Can one go farther? Ambiguity expresses being as dissimulated; it says that being is, insofar as it is dissimulated. For being to accomplish its work, it must be dissimulated: it works by dissimulating itself, it is always reserved and preserved by dissimulation, but also subjected to it; dissimulation then tends to become the purity of negation. But at the same time, ambiguity, when everything is dissimulated, says (and this saying is ambiguity itself): all being *is* through dissimulation, being is essentially being in the heart of dissimulation.

Ambiguity, then, no longer consists only of the incessant movement through which being returns to nothingness and nothingness refers back to being. Ambiguity is no longer the primordial Yes and No in which being and nothingness are pure identity. Essential ambiguity lies rather in the fact that—before the beginning—nothingness is not equal to being, is only the *appearance* of the dissimulation of being, or else that dissimulation is more "original" than negation. So that one could say: *ambiguity is essential in inverse proportion to the capacity of dissimulation to recapture itself in negation.*

Reading

Reading: we are not surprised to find admissions like this in a writer's travel diary: "Always such dread at the moment of writing . . . " and when Lomazzo talks about the horror that seized Leonardo every time he tried to paint, we can understand this, too, we feel we could understand it.

But if a person confided to us, "I am always anxious at the moment of reading," or another could not read except at rare, special times, or another would disrupt his whole life, renounce the world, forego work and happiness in the world, in order to open the way for himself to a few moments of reading, we would undoubtedly place him alongside Pierre Janet's patient who was reluctant to read because, she said, "when a book is read it becomes dirty."

The person who enjoys simply listening to music becomes a musician as he listens, and the same kind of thing happens when someone looks at paintings. The world of music and the world of painting can be entered by anyone who has the key to them. That key is the "gift," and the gift is the enchantment and understanding of a certain taste. Lovers of music and lovers of painting are people who openly display their preference like a delectable ailment that isolates them and makes them proud. The others modestly recognize the fact that they have no ear. One must be gifted to hear and to see. This gift is a closed space—the concert hall, the museum—with which one surrounds oneself in order to enjoy a clandestine pleasure. People who do not have the gift remain outside, people who have it go in and out as they please. Naturally, music is loved only on Sunday; this god is no more demanding than the other.

Reading does not even require any gift, and it refutes that recourse to a natural privilege. No one is gifted—not the author, not the reader—and anyone who feels he is gifted primarily feels he is not gifted, feels that he is infinitely unequipped, that he lacks the power attributed to him, and just as being an "artist" means not knowing there is already an art, not knowing there is already a world, so reading, seeing, and hearing works of art demands more ignorance than knowledge, it demands a knowledge filled with immense ignorance, and a gift that is not given beforehand, a gift that is received, secured and lost each time in self-forgetfulness. Each picture, each piece of music presents us with the organ we need in order to receive it, "gives" us the eye and the ear we need in order to see it and hear it. Nonmusicians are people who decide in the very beginning to reject the possibility of hearing, they hide from it as though suspiciously closing themselves off from a threat or an irritation. André Breton repudiates music, because he wants to preserve within himself his right to hear the discordant essence of language, its nonmusical music, and Kafka, who constantly recognizes that he is more closed to music than anyone else in the world, manages to regard this defect as one of his strong points: "I am really strong, I have one particular strength, and that is— to characterize it in a brief and unclear manner—my nonmusical being."

Usually someone who does not like music cannot tolerate it at all, just as a man who finds a Picasso painting repellent excludes it with a violent hatred, as though he felt directly threatened by it. The fact that he hasn't even looked at the picture says nothing against his good faith. It is not in his power to look at it. Not looking at it does not put him in the wrong, it is a form of his sincerity, his correct presentiment of the force that is closing his eyes. "I refuse to look at that." "I could not live with that before my eyes." These formulations define the hidden reality of the work of art—its absolute intolerance—more powerfully than the art lover's suspect complacencies. It is quite true that one cannot live with a picture before one's eyes.

The plastic work of art has a certain advantage over the verbal work of art in that it renders more manifest the exclusive void within which the work apparently wants to remain, far from everyone's gaze. Rodin's "The Kiss" allows itself to be looked at and even thrives on being looked at; his "Balzac" is without gaze, a closed and sleeping thing, absorbed in itself to such a degree that it disappears. This decisive separation, which sculpture takes as its element and which sets out another, rebellious space in the center of space—sets out a space that is at once hidden, visible, and shielded, perhaps immutable, perhaps without repose—this protected violence, before which we always feel out of place, does not seem to be present in books. The statue that is unearthed and displayed for everyone's admiration does not expect anything, does not receive anything, seems rather to have been torn from its place. But isn't it true that the book that has been exhumed, the manuscript that is taken out of a jar and enters the broad daylight of reading, is born all over again through an impressive piece of luck? What is a book that no one reads? Something that has not yet been written. Reading, then, is not writing the book again but causing the book to write itself or *be* written—this time without the writer as intermediary, without anyone writing it. The reader does not add himself to the book, but his tendency is first to unburden it of any author, and something very hasty in his approach, the very futile shadow that passes across the pages and leaves them intact, everything that makes the reading appear superfluous, and even the reader's lack of attention, the slightness of his interest, all his infinite lightness affirms the book's new lightness: the book has become a book without an author, without the seriousness, the labor, the heavy pangs, the weight of a whole life that has been poured into it—an experience that is sometimes terrible, always dangerous, an experience the reader effaces and, because of his providential lightness, considers to be nothing.

Although he does not know it, the reader is involved in a profound struggle with the author: no matter how much intimacy remains today between the book and the writer, no matter how directly the author's figure, presence, and history are illuminated by the circumstances of publication—circumstances that are not accidental but that may be already slightly anachronistic—in spite of this, every reading in which consideration of the writer seems to play such a large role is an impeachment that obliterates him in order to give the work back to itself, to its anonymous presence, to the violent, impersonal affirmation that it is. The reader himself is always fundamentally anonymous, he is any reader, unique but transparent. Instead of adding his name to the book (as our fathers did in the past), he rather erases all names by his nameless presence, by that modest, passive, interchangeable, insignificant gaze under whose gentle pressure the book appears written, at one remove from everything and everyone.

Reading transforms a book the same way the sea and the wind transform the works of men: the result is a smoother stone, a fragment that has fallen from heaven, without any past, without any future, and that we do not wonder about as we look at it. Reading endows the book with the kind of sudden existence that the statue "seems" to take from the chisel alone: the isolation that hides it from eyes that see it, the proud remoteness, the orphan wisdom that drives off the sculptor just as much as it does the look that tries to sculpt it again. In some sense the book needs the reader in order to become a statue, it needs the reader in order to assert itself as a thing without an author and also without a reader. What reading brings to it is not first of all a more human truth; but neither does it make the book into something inhuman, an "object," a pure compact presence, fruit from the depths unripened by our sun. It simply "makes" the book—the work—become a work beyond the person who produced it, beyond the experience expressed in it and even beyond all the artistic resources that various traditions have made available. The nature of reading, its singularity, illuminates the singular meaning of the verb "to make" in the expression "it makes the work become a work." Here the word "make" does not indicate a productive activity: reading does not make anything, does not add anything; it lets be what is; it is freedom—not the kind of freedom that gives being or takes it away, but a liberty that receives, consents, says yes, can only say yes, and in the space opened by this yes, allows the work's amazing decision to be affirmed: that it is—and nothing more.

"Lazare, veni foras."

Reading that accepts the work for what it is and in so doing unburdens it of its author, does not consist of replacing the author by a reader, a fully existent person, who has a history, a profession, a religion, and is even well read, someone who, on the basis of all that, would begin a dialogue with the other person, the one who wrote the book. Reading is not a conversation, it does not discuss, it does not question. It never asks the book—and certainly not the author—"What exactly did you mean?

Well, what truth are you offering me?" True reading never challenges the true book: but it is not a form of submission to the "text" either. Only the nonliterary book is presented as a stoutly woven web of determined significations, as an entity made up of real affirmations: before it is read by anyone, the nonliterary book has already been read by everyone, and it is this preliminary reading that guarantees it a secure existence. But the book whose source is art has no guarantee in the world, and when it is read, it has never been read before; it only attains its presence as a work in the space opened by this unique reading, each time the first reading and each time the only reading.

This is the source of the strange freedom exemplified by reading, literary reading. It is free movement, if it is not subject to anything, if it does not depend on anything already present. The book is undoubtedly there—not only in its reality as paper and print, but also in its nature as a book, this fabric of stable significations, this affirmation that it owes to a · preestablished language, and also this precinct formed around it by the community of all readers, which already includes me even though I have not read it, and also made up of all other books, which, like angels with interlaced wings, watch closely over the unknown volume, because if even one book is threatened, a dangerous breach is opened in the world's library. And so the book is there, but the work is still hidden, perhaps radically absent, in any case disguised, obscured by the obviousness of the book behind which it awaits the liberating decision, the *Lazare, veni foras.*

The mission of reading seems to be to cause this stone to fall: to make it transparent, to dissolve it with the penetration of a gaze which enthusiastically goes beyond it. There is something dizzying about reading, or at least about the outset of reading, that resembles the irrational impulse by which we try to open eyes that are already closed, open them to life; this impulse is connected to desire, which is a leap, an infinite leap, just as inspiration is a leap: I want to *read* what has nevertheless not been written. But there is more, and what makes the "miracle" of reading—which perhaps enlightens us concerning the meaning of all thaumaturgy—even more singular is that here the stone and the tomb not only contain a cadaverous emptiness that must be animated, but they also constitute the presence—hidden though it is—of what must appear. To roll the stone, to move it away, is certainly something marvellous, but we accomplish it each instant in our everyday language, and we converse each instant with this Lazarus, who has been dead for three days, or perhaps forever, and who, beneath his tightly woven bandages, is sustained by the most elegant conventions, and answers us and talks to us in our very hearts. But what responds to the appeal of literary reading is not a door falling or becoming transparent or even becoming a little thinner; rather, it is a rougher kind of stone, more tightly sealed, crushing—a vast deluge of stone that shakes the earth and the sky.

Such is the particular nature of this "opening," which is what reading is made up of: only what is more tightly closed opens; only what has been borne as an oppressive nothingness without consistency can be admitted into the lightness of a free and happy Yes. And this does not tie the poetic work to the search for an obscurity that would confound everyday understanding. It merely establishes a violent rupture between the book that is there and the work that is never there beforehand, between the book that is the concealed work and the work that cannot affirm itself except in the thickness—thickness made present—of this concealment: it establishes a violent rupture, and the passage from a world in which everything has some degree of meaning, in which there is darkness and light, to a space where nothing has any meaning yet, properly speaking, but to which, even so, everything that has meaning returns as to its own origin.

But these remarks would also risk deceiving us, if they seemed to say that reading was the work of clearing a way from one language to another, or a bold step requiring initiative, effort, and the conquest of obstacles. The approach to reading may be a difficult kind of happiness, but reading is the easiest thing in the world, it is freedom without work, a pure Yes blossoming in the immediate.

The light, innocent Yes of reading.

Reading, in the sense of literary reading, is not even a pure movement of comprehension, the kind of understanding that tries to sustain meaning by setting it in motion again. Reading is situated beyond comprehension or short of comprehension. Nor is reading exactly an appeal that the unique work that should disclose itself in reading reveal itself behind the appearance of common speech, behind the book that belongs to everyone. No doubt there is some sort of appeal, but it can only come from the work itself, it is a silent appeal that imposes silence in the midst of the general noise, an appeal the reader hears only as he responds to it, that deflects the reader from his habitual relations and turns him towards the space near which reading bides and becomes an approach, a delighted reception of the generosity of the work, a reception that raises the book to the work that it is, through the same rapture that raises the work to being and turns the reception into a ravishment, the ravishment in which the work is articulated. Reading is this abode and it has the simplicity of the light and transparent Yes that is this abode. Even if it demands that the reader enter a zone in which he has no air and the ground is hidden from him, even if, beyond these stormy approaches, reading seems to be a kind of participation in the open violence that is the work, in itself reading is a tranquil and silent presence, the pacified center of excess, the silent Yes that lies at the heart of every storm.

The freedom of this Yes—which is present, ravished, and transparent—is the essence of reading. Because of this, reading stands in contrast to that aspect of the work which, through the experience of creation, approaches absence, the torments of the infinite, the empty depths of something that never begins or ends—a movement that exposes the creator to the threat of essential solitude, that delivers him to the interminable.

In this sense, reading is more positive than creation, more creative, although it does not produce anything. It shares in the decision, it has the lightness, the irresponsibility, the innocence of the decision. It does nothing and everything is accomplished. For Kafka there was dread, there were unfinished stories, the torment of a wasted life, of a mission betrayed, every day turned into an exile, every night exiled from sleep, and finally, there was the certainty that "The Metamorphosis is unreadable, radically flawed." But for Kafka's reader, the dread turns into ease and happiness, the torment over faults is transfigured into innocence, and in each scrap of text there is delight in fullness, certainty of completion, a revelation of the unique, inevitable, unpredictable work. This is the essence of reading, of the light Yes which—far more effectively than the creator's dark struggle with chaos, in which he seeks to disappear so as to master it—evokes the divine share of creation.

This is why an author's grievances against the reader often seem misplaced. Montesquieu writes, "I am asking a favor that I am afraid no one will grant me: and that is not to judge twenty years' work in a moment's reading; to approve or condemn the entire book and not just a few sentences," and he is asking something that artists are often sorry they do not have, as they think with bitterness how their works are the victims of a casual reading, a distracted glance, a careless ear: such effort, such sacrifice, such care, such calculation, a life of solitude, centuries of meditation and seeking—all this is appraised, judged and annihilated by the ignorant decision of the first person to come along, by a chance mood. And when Valéry worries about today's uncultivated reader who demands that facility accompany his reading, this worry may be justified, but the culture of an attentive reader, the scruples of a reading filled with devotion, an almost religious reading, one that has become a sort of cult, would not change anything; it would create even more serious dangers, because although the lightness of a casual reader, dancing quickly around the text, may not be true lightness, it has no consequences and holds a certain promise: it proclaims the happiness and innocence of reading, which may in fact be a dance with an invisible partner in a separate space, a joyful, wild dance with the "tomb." Lightness from which we must not hope for the impulse of a graver concern, because where we have lightness, gravity is not lacking.

The Gaze of Orpheus

When Orpheus descends to Eurydice, art is the power that causes the night to open. Because of the power of art, the night welcomes him; it becomes the welcoming intimacy, the understanding and the harmony of the first night. But Orpheus has gone down to Eurydice: for him, Eurydice is the limit of what art can attain; concealed behind a name and covered by a veil, she is the profoundly dark point towards which art, desire, death, and the night all seem to lead. She is the instant in which the essence of the night approaches as the *other* night.

Yet Orpheus' work does not consist of securing the approach of this "point" by descending into the depths. His *work* is to bring it back into the daylight and in the daylight give it form, figure and reality. Orpheus can do anything except look this "point" in the face, look at the center of the night in the night. He can descend to it, he can draw it to him—an even stronger power—and he can draw it upwards, but only by keeping his back turned to it. This turning away is the only way he can approach it: this is the meaning of the concealment revealed in the night. But in the impulse of his migration Orpheus forgets the work he has to accomplish, and he has to forget it, because the ultimate requirement of his impulse is not that there should be a work, but that someone should stand and face this "point" and grasp its essence where this essence appears, where it is essential and essentially appearance: in the heart of the night.

The Greek myth says: one cannot create a work unless the enormous experience of the depths—an experience which the Greeks recognized as necessary to the work, an experience in which the work is put to the test by that enormousness—is not pursued for its own sake. The depth does not surrender itself face to face; it only reveals itself by concealing itself in the work. A fundamental, inexorable answer. But the myth also shows that Orpheus' destiny is not to submit to that law—and it is certainly true that by turning around to look at Eurydice, Orpheus ruins the work, the work immediately falls apart, and Eurydice returns to the shadows; under his gaze, the essence of the night reveals itself to be inessential. He thus betrays the work and Eurydice and the night. But if he did not turn around to look at Eurydice, he still would be betraying, being disloyal to, the boundless and imprudent force of his impulse, which does not demand Eurydice in her diurnal truth and her everyday charm, but in her nocturnal darkness, in her distance, her body closed, her face sealed, which wants to see her not when she is visible, but when she is invisible, and not as the intimacy of a familiar life, but as the strangeness of that which excludes all intimacy; it does not want to make her live, but to have the fullness of her death living in her.

It is only this that he has come to look for in Hell. The whole glory of his work, the whole power of his art and even the desire for a happy life in the beautiful light of day are sacrificed to this one concern: to look into the night at what the night is concealing—the *other* night, concealment which becomes visible.

This is an infinitely problematical impulse which the day condemns as an unjustifiable act of madness or as the expiation of excess. For the day, this descent into Hell, this impulse toward the empty depths, is already excessive. It is inevitable that Orpheus defy the law forbidding him to "turn around," because he has already violated it the moment he takes his first step towards the shadows. This observation makes us sense that Orpheus has actually been turned towards Eurydice all along: he saw her when she was invisible and he touched her intact, in her absence as a shade, in that veiled presence which did not conceal her absence, which was the presence of her infinite absence. If he had not looked at her, he would not have drawn her to him, and no doubt she is not there, but he himself is absent in this glance, he is no less dead than she was, not dead with the tranquil death of the world, the kind of death which is repose, silence, and ending, but with that other death which is endless death, proof of the absence of ending.

Passing judgment on what Orpheus undertakes to do, the day also reproaches him for having shown impatience. Orpheus' mistake, then, would seem to lie in the desire which leads him to see Eurydice and to possess her, while he is destined only to sing about her. He is only Orpheus in his song, he could have no relationship with Eurydice except within the hymn, he has life and actuality only after the poem and through the poem, and Eurydice represents nothing more than that magical dependence which makes him into a shade when he is not singing and only allows him to be free, alive, and powerful within the space of the Orphic measure. Yes, this much is true: only in the song does Orpheus have power over Eurydice, but in the song Eurydice is also already lost and Orpheus himself is the scattered Orpheus, the "infinitely dead" Orpheus into which the power of the song transforms him from then on. He loses Eurydice because he desires her beyond the measured limits of the song, and he loses himself too, but this desire, and Eurydice lost, and Orpheus scattered are necessary to the song, just as the ordeal of eternal worklessness is necessary to the work.

Orpheus is guilty of impatience. His error is that he wants to exhaust the infinite, that he puts an end to what is unending, that he does not endlessly sustain the very impulse of his error. Impatience is the mistake made by a person who wishes to escape the absence of time; patience is the trick that tries to master this absence of time by turning it into another kind of time, measured in a different way. But true patience does not exclude impatience; it is the heart of impatience, it is impatience endlessly suffered and endured. Orpheus' impatience is therefore also a correct impulse: it is the source of what will become his own passion, his highest patience, his infinite sojourn in death.

Inspiration.

Although the world may judge Orpheus, the work does not judge him, does not point out his faults. The work says nothing. And everything happens as if, by disobeying the law, by looking at Eurydice, Orpheus was only yielding to the profound demands of the work, as though, through this inspired gesture, he really had carried the dark shade out of Hell, as though he had unknowingly brought it back into the broad daylight of the work.

To look at Eurydice without concern for the song, in the impatience and imprudence of a desire which forgets the law—this is *inspiration*.

Does this mean that inspiration changes the beauty of the night into the unreality of the void, makes Eurydice into a shade and Orpheus into someone infinitely dead? Does it mean that inspiration is therefore that problematic moment when the essence of the night becomes something inessential and the welcoming intimacy of the first night becomes the deceptive trap of the *other* night? This is exactly the way it is. All we can sense of inspiration is its failure, all we can recognize of it is its misguided violence. But if inspiration means that Orpheus fails and Eurydice is lost twice over, if it means the insignificance and void of the night, it also turns Orpheus towards that failure and that insignificance and coerces him, by an irresistible impulse, as though giving up failure were much more serious than giving up success, as though what we call the insignificant, the inessential, the mistaken, could reveal itself—to someone who accepted the risk and freely gave himself up to it—as the source of all authenticity.

His inspired and forbidden gaze dooms Orpheus to lose everything— not only himself, not only the gravity of the day, but also the essence of the night: this much is certain, inevitable. Inspiration means the ruin of Orpheus and the certainty of his ruin, and it does not promise the success of the work as compensation, anymore than in the work it affirms Orpheus' ideal triumph or Eurydice's survival. The work is just as much compromised by inspiration as Orpheus is threatened by it. In that instant it reaches its extreme point of uncertainty. This is why it so often and so strongly resists what inspires it. This is also why it protects itself by saying to Orpheus: "You will only be able to keep me if you do not look at *her.*" But this forbidden act is precisely the one Orpheus must perform in order to take the work beyond what guarantees it, and which he can perform only by forgetting the work, carried away by a desire coming out of the night and bound to the night as its origin. In this respect, the work is lost. This is the only moment when it is absolutely lost, when something more important than the work, more stripped of importance than the work, is proclaimed and asserted. The work is everything to Orpheus, everything except that desired gaze in which the work is lost, so that it is also only in this gaze that the work can go beyond itself, unite with its origin and establish itself in impossibility.

Orpheus' gaze is Orpheus' ultimate gift to the work, a gift in which he rejects the work, in which he sacrifices it by moving towards its origin in the boundless impulse of desire, and in which he unknowingly still moves towards the work, towards the origin of the work.

For Orpheus, then, everything sinks into the certainty of failure, where the only remaining compensation is the uncertainty of the work—for does the work ever exist? As we look at the most certain masterpiece, whose beginning dazzles us with its brilliance and decisiveness, we find that we are also faced with something which is fading away, a work that has suddenly become invisible again, is no longer there, and has never been there. This sudden eclipse is the distant memory of Orpheus' gaze, it is a nostalgic return to the uncertainty of the origin.

Gift and sacrifice.

If forced to stress what such a moment seems to reveal about inspiration, we would have to say: it connects inspiration with *desire*.

It introduces into the concern for the work the gesture of *unconcern* in which the work is sacrificed: the last law of the work has been transgressed, the work has been betrayed for the sake of Eurydice, the shade. This unconcern is the movement of sacrifice, a sacrifice which can only be unconcerned, thoughtless, which is perhaps a failing, is immediately atoned for as though it were a failing, but whose substance is thoughtlessness, unconcern, innocence: an unceremonious sacrifice in which the unconcerned gaze which is not even a sacrilege, which has none of the heaviness or gravity of an act of profanation, returned the sacred itself—night in its unapproachable depth—to the inessential, which is not the profane but rather does not fall within these categories.

The essential night which follows Orpheus—before the careless look—the sacred night which he holds enthralled in the fascination of his song and which is at that point kept within the limits and the measured space of the song, is certainly richer, more august, than the empty futility which it becomes after Orpheus looks back. The sacred night encloses Eurydice, encloses within the song something which went beyond the song. But it is also enclosed itself: it is bound, it is the attendant, it is the sacred mastered by the power of ritual—that word which means order, rectitude, law, the way of Tao and the axis of Dharma. Orpheus' gaze unties it, destroys its limits, breaks the law which contains, which retains the essence. Thus Orpheus' gaze is the extreme moment of freedom, the moment in which he frees himself of himself and—what is more important—frees the work of his concern, frees the sacred contained in the work, *gives* the sacred to itself, to the freedom of its essence, to its essence which is freedom (for this reason, inspiration is the greatest gift). So everything is at stake in the decision of the gaze. In this decision, the origin is approached by the force of the gaze, which sets free the essence of the night, removes concern, interrupts the incessant by revealing it: a moment of desire, unconcern, and authority.

Inspiration is bound to *desire* by Orpheus' gaze. Desire is bound to *unconcern* by *impatience*. A person who is not impatient will never reach the point of being unconcerned—that moment when concern merges with its own transparency; but a person who does not get beyond impatience will never be capable of Orpheus' unconcerned, thoughtless gaze. This is why impatience must be the heart of deep patience, the pure bolt of lightning which leaps out of the breast of patience because of its infinite waiting, its silence, and its reserve, not only as a spark lit by extreme tension, but also like the glittering point which has eluded that waiting: the happy chance of unconcern.

The leap.

The act of writing begins with Orpheus' gaze, and that gaze is the impulse of desire which shatters the song's destiny and concern, and in that inspired and unconcerned decision reaches the origin, consecrates the song. But Orpheus already needed the power of art in order to descend to that instant. This means: one can only write if one arrives at the instant towards which one can only move through space opened up by the movement of writing. In order to write one must already be writing. The essence of writing, the difficulty of experience and the leap of inspiration also lie within this contradiction.

The Song of the Sirens
Encountering the Imaginary

The Sirens: evidently they really sang, but in a way that was not satisfying, that only implied in which direction lay the true sources of the song, the true happiness of the song. Nevertheless, through their imperfect songs, songs which were only a song still to come, they guided the sailor towards that space where singing would really begin. They were therefore not deceiving him; they were really leading him to his goal. But what happened when he reached that place? What was that place? It was a place where the only thing left was to disappear, because in this region of source and origin, music itself had disappeared more completely than in any other place in the world; it was like a sea into which the living would sink with their ears closed and where the Sirens, too, even they, as proof of their good will, would one day have to disappear.

What sort of song was the Sirens' song? What was its defect? Why did this defect make it so powerful? The answer some people have always given is that it was an inhuman song—no doubt a natural noise (what other kind is there?), but one that remained in the margins of nature; in any case, it was foreign to man, and very low, awakening in him that extreme delight in falling which he cannot satisfy in the normal conditions of his life. But, others say, there was something even stranger in the enchantment: it caused the Sirens merely to reproduce the ordinary singing of mankind, and because the Sirens, who were only animals— very beautiful animals because they reflected womanly beauty—could sing the way men sing, their song became so extraordinary that it created in anyone who heard it a suspicion that all human singing was really inhuman. Was it despair, then, that killed men moved to passion by their own singing? That despair verged upon rapture. There was something marvellous about the song: it actually existed, it was ordinary and at the same time secret, a simple, everyday song which they were suddenly forced to recognize, sung in an unreal way by strange powers, powers which were, in a word, imaginary; it was a song from the abyss and once heard it opened an abyss in every utterance and powerfully enticed whoever heard it to disappear into that abyss.

Remember that this song was sung to sailors, men prepared to take risks and fearless in their impulses, and it was a form of navigation too: it was a distance, and what it revealed was the possibility of traveling that distance, of making the song into a movement towards the song and of making this movement into the expression of the greatest desire. Strange navigation, and what was its goal? It has always been possible to believe that those who approached it were not able to do more than approach it, that they died from impatience, from having said too soon: "Here it is; here is where I will drop anchor." Others have claimed that, on the contrary, it was too late: the goal had always been overshot; the enchantment held out an enigmatic promise and through this promise exposed men to the danger of being unfaithful to themselves, unfaithful to their human song and even to the essence of song, by awakening in them hope and the desire for a marvellous beyond, and that beyond was only a desert, as though the region where music originated was the only place completely without music, a sterile dry place where silence, like noise, burned all access to the song in anyone who had once had command of it. Does this mean that there was something evil in the invitation which issued from the depths? Were the Sirens nothing more than unreal voices, as custom would have us believe, unreal voices which were not supposed to be heard, a deception intended to seduce, and which could only be resisted by disloyal or cunning people?

Men have always made a rather ignoble effort to discredit the Sirens by accusing them flatly of lying: they were liars when they sang, frauds when they sighed, fictions when they were touched—nonexistent in every way; and the good sense of Ulysses was enough to do away with this puerile nonexistence.

It is true, Ulysses did overcome them, but how did he do it? Ulysses—the stubbornness and caution of Ulysses, the treachery by which he took pleasure in the spectacle of the Sirens without risking anything and without accepting the consequences; this cowardly, mediocre and tranquil pleasure, this moderate pleasure, appropriate to a Greek of the period of decadence who never deserved to be the hero of the *Iliad*; this happy and confident cowardice, rooted in a privilege which set him apart from the common condition, the others having no right to such elite happiness but only to the pleasure of seeing their leader writhe ludicrously, grimacing with ecstasy in empty space, but also a right to the satisfaction of gaining mastery over their master (no doubt this was the lesson they learned, this was for them the true song of the Sirens): Ulysses' attitude, the amazing deafness of a man who is deaf because he can hear, was enough to fill the Sirens with a despair which until then had been felt only by men, and this despair turned them into real and beautiful girls, just this once real and worthy of their promise, and therefore capable of vanishing into the truth and depth of their song.

Even once the Sirens had been overcome by the power of technology, which will always claim to trifle in safety with unreal (inspired) powers, Ulysses was still not free of them. They enticed him to a place which he did not want to fall into and, hidden in the heart of *The Odyssey*, which had become their tomb, they drew him—and many others—into that happy, unhappy voyage which is the voyage of the tale—of a song which is no longer immediate, but is narrated, and because of this made to seem harmless, an ode which has turned into an episode.

The secret law of the tale.

This is not an allegory. A very obscure struggle takes place between every tale and the encounter with the Sirens, that enigmatic song which is powerful because of its insufficiency. A struggle in which Ulysses' prudence—whatever degree he has of truth, of mystification, of obstinate ability not to play the game of the gods—has always been exercised and perfected. What we call the novel was born of this struggle. What lies in the foreground of the novel is the previous voyage, the voyage which takes Ulysses to the moment of the encounter. This voyage is a completely human story, it takes place within the framework of human time, it is bound up with men's passions; it actually takes place and is rich enough and varied enough to consume all the narrators' strength and attention. Once the tale has become a novel, far from appearing poorer it takes on all the richness and breadth of an exploration, one which sometimes embraces the immensity of the voyage and sometimes confines itself to a small patch of space on the deck and occasionally descends into the depths of the ship where no one ever knew what the hope of the sea was. The rule the sailors must obey is this: no allusion can be made to a goal or a destination. And with good reason, surely. No one can sail away with the deliberate intention of reaching the Isle of Capri, no one can set his course for it, and if anyone decides to go there he will still proceed only by chance, by some chance to which he is linked by an understanding difficult to penetrate. The rule is therefore silence, discretion, forgetfulness.

We must recognize that a certain preordained modesty, a desire not to have any pretensions and not to lead to anything, would be enough to make many novels irreproachable books and to make the genre of the novel the most attractive of genres, the one which, in its discretion and its cheerful nothingness, takes upon itself the task of forgetting what others degrade by calling it the essential. Diversion is its profound song. To keep changing direction, to move on in an apparently random way, avoiding all goals, with an uneasy motion that is transformed into a happy sort of distraction—this has been its primary and most secure justification. It is no small thing to make a game of human time and out of that game to create a free occupation, one stripped of all immediate interest and usefulness, essentially superficial and yet in its surface movement capable of absorbing all being. But clearly, if the novel fails to play this role today, it is because technics has transformed men's time and their ways of amusing themselves.

The tale begins at a point where the novel does not go, though in its refusals and its rich neglect it is leading towards it. Heroically, pretentiously, the tale is the tale of one single episode, that in which Ulysses encounters the inadequate and enticing song of the Sirens. Except for this great, naive pretension, apparently nothing has changed, and because of its form the tale seems to continue to fulfill its ordinary vocation as a narrative. For example, *Aurélia* is presented as the simple account of a meeting, and so is *Une saison en Enfer,* and so is *Nadja.*

Something has happened, something which someone has experienced who tells about it afterwards, in the same way that Ulysses needed to experience the event and survive it in order to become Homer, who told about it. Of course the tale is usually about an exceptional event, one which eludes the forms of everyday time and the world of the usual sort of truth, perhaps any truth. This is why it so insistently rejects everything which could connect it with the frivolity of a fiction (the novel, on the other hand, contains only what is believable and familiar and yet is very anxious to pass for fiction). In the *Gorgias*, Plato says "Listen to a beautiful tale. Now you will think it is a fable, but I believe it is a tale. I will tell you what I am going to tell you as a true thing." What he told was the story of the Last Judgment.

Yet if we regard the tale as the true telling of an exceptional event which has taken place and which someone is trying to report, then we have not even come close to sensing the true nature of the tale. The tale is not the narration of an event, but that event itself, the approach to that event, the place where that event is made to happen—an event which is yet to come and through whose power of attraction the tale can hope to come into being, too.

This is a very delicate relationship, undoubtedly a kind of extravagance, but it is the secret law of the tale. The tale is a movement towards a point, a point which is not only unknown, obscure, foreign, but such that apart from this movement it does not seem to have any sort of real prior existence, and yet it is so imperious that the tale derives its power of attraction only from this point, so that it cannot even "begin" before reaching it—and yet only the tale and the unpredictable movement of the tale create the space where the point becomes real, powerful, and alluring.

When Ulysses becomes Homer.

What would happen if instead of being two distinct people Ulysses and Homer comfortably shared their roles, and were one and the same presence? If the tale Homer told were simply Ulysses' movement within the space opened up for him by the Song of the Sirens? If Homer's capacity to narrate were limited by how far he went as Ulysses—a

Ulysses free of all impediments, though tied down—towards the place where the power to speak and to narrate was apparently promised to him as long as he disappeared there?

This is one of the strange things about the tale, or shall we say one of its pretensions. It only "narrates" itself, and in the same moment that this narration comes into being it creates what it is narrating; it cannot exist as a narration unless it creates what is happening in that narration, because then it contains the point or the plane where the reality "described" by the story can keep uniting with its reality as a tale, can secure this reality and be secured by it.

But isn't this a rather naive madness? In one sense, yes. That is why there are no tales, and that is why there is no lack of tales.

To listen to the Song of the Sirens is to cease to be Ulysses and become Homer, but only in Homer's story does the real encounter take place, where Ulysses becomes the one who enters into a relationship with the force of the elements and the voice of the abyss.

This seems obscure, it is like the embarrassment the first man would have felt if, in order to be created, he himself had had to pronounce in a completely human way the divine *Fiat lux* that would actually cause his eyes to open.

Actually, this way of presenting things simplifies them a great deal—which is why it produces these artificial or theoretical complications. Of course it is true that only in Melville's book does Ahab meet Moby Dick; yet it is also true that only this encounter allows Melville to write the book, it is such an imposing encounter, so enormous, so special that it goes beyond all the levels on which it takes place, all the moments in time where we attempt to situate it, and seems to be happening long before the book begins, but it is of such a nature that it also could not happen more than once, in the future of the work and in that sea which is what the work will be, having become an ocean on its own scale.

Ahab and the whale are engaged in a drama, what we can call a metaphysical drama, using the word loosely, and the Sirens and Ulysses are engaged in the same struggle. Each wants to be everything, wants to be the absolute world, which would make it impossible for him to coexist with the other absolute world, and yet the greatest desire of each is for this coexistence and this encounter. To bring Ahab and the whale, the Sirens and Ulysses together in one space—this is the secret wish which turns Ulysses into Homer and Ahab into Melville, and makes the world that results from this union into the greatest, most terrible, and most beautiful of all possible worlds: a book, alas, only a book.

Of Ahab and Ulysses, the one with the greater will to power is not the more liberated. Ulysses has the kind of deliberate stubbornness which leads to universal domination: his trick is to seem to limit his power; in a cold and calculating way he finds out what he can still do, faced with the other power. He will be everything, if he can maintain a limit, if he can preserve that interval between the real and the imaginary which is just what the Song of the Sirens invites him to cross. The result is a sort of victory for him, a dark disaster for Ahab. We cannot deny that Ulysses understood something of what Ahab saw, but he stood fast within that understanding, while Ahab became lost in the image. In other words, one resisted the metamorphosis while the other entered it and disappeared inside it. After the test, Ulysses is just as he had been before, and the world is poorer, perhaps, but firmer and more sure. Ahab is no longer, and for Melville himself the world keeps threatening to sink into that worldless space towards which the fascination of one single image draws him.

The metamorphosis.

The tale is bound up with the metamorphosis alluded to by Ulysses and Ahab. The action that the tale causes to take place in the present is that of metamorphosis on all the levels it can attain. If for the sake of convenience—because this statement cannot be exact— we say that what makes the novel move forward is everyday, collective or personal time, or more precisely, the desire to urge time to speak, then the tale moves forward through that *other* time, it makes that other voyage, which is the passage from the real song to the imaginary song, the movement which causes the real song to become imaginary little by little, though all at once (and this "little by little, though all at once" is the very time of the metamorphosis), to become an enigmatic song always at a distance, designating this distance as a space to be crossed and designating the place to which it leads as the point where singing will cease to be a lure.

The tale wants to cross this space, and what moves it is the transformation demanded by the empty fullness of this space, a transformation which takes place in all directions and no doubt powerfully transforms the writer but transforms the tale itself no less and everything at stake in the tale, where in a sense nothing happens except this very crossing. And yet what was more important for Melville than the encounter with Moby Dick, an encounter which is taking place now and is "at the same time" always imminent, so that he keeps moving towards it in a stubborn and disorderly quest, but since this encounter is just as closely related to the source, it also seems to be sending him back into the depths of the past—Proust lived under the fascination of this experience and in part succeeded in writing under it.

People will object, saying: but the events they are talking about belong primarily to the "lives" of Melville, Nerval, Proust. It is because they have already met Aurélia, because they have tripped over the uneven paving stones, seen the three church towers, that they can begin to form, an image, a story, or words—that will let us share a vision close to their own vision. Unfortunately, things are not that simple. All the ambiguity arises from the ambiguity of time which comes into place here and which allows us to say and to feel that the fascinating image of the experience is present at a certain moment, even though this presence does not belong to any present, and even destroys the present which it seems to enter. It is true, Ulysses was really sailing, and one day, on a certain date, he encountered the enigmatic song. And so he can say: now—this is happening now. But what happened now? The presence of a song which was still to be sung. And what did he touch in the presence? Not the occurence of an encounter which had become present, but the overture of the infinite movement which is the encounter itself, always at a distance from the place where it asserts itself and the moment when it asserts itself, because it is this very distance, this imaginary distance, in which absence is realized, and only at the end of this distance does the event begin to take place, at a point where the proper truth of the encounter comes into being and where, in any case, the words which speak it would originate.

Always still to come, always in the past already, always present— beginning so abruptly that it takes your breath away—and yet unfurling itself like the eternal return and renewal—"*Ah,*" says Goethe, "*in another age you were my sister or my wife*"—this is the nature of the event for which the tale is the approach. This event upsets relations in time, and yet affirms time, the particular way time happens, the tale's own time which enters the narrator's duration in such a way as to transform it, and the time of the metamorphoses where the different temporal ecstasies coincide in an imaginary simultaneity and in the form of the space which art is trying to create.

The Power and the Glory

I would like to make a few brief and simple statements that may help us to situate literature and the writer.

There was a time when a writer, like an artist, had some relation to glory. Glorification was his work, glory was the gift he gave and received. Glory in the ancient sense is the radiance of a presence (sacred or royal). And Rilke, too, says that to glorify does not mean to make known; glory is the manifestation of being as it advances in its magnificence as being, free of what conceals it, secure in the truth of its exposed presence.

Glory is followed by renown. Renown applies more exactly to the name. The power of naming, the force of what denominates, the dangerous assurance of the name (there is danger in being named) become the privilege of the person who can name and make what he names be understood. Understanding is subject to notoriety. Speech eternalized in writing promises immortality. The writer has thrown in his lot with what triumphs over death; he knows nothing of what is temporary; he is the friend of the soul, a man of the spirit, guarantor of what is eternal. Even today, many critics seem to believe sincerely that the vocation of art and literature is to eternalize man.

Renown is succeeded by reputation, just as the truth is succeeded by opinion. The fact of publishing—publication—becomes the essential thing. This can be taken in a superficial sense: the writer is known to the public, he has a large reputation, he wants to become prominent, highly valued, because he needs value—which is money. But value is procured by the public, and what excites the public? Publicity. Publicity becomes an art in itself, it is the art of all the arts, it is what is most important, since it determines the power that gives determination to everything else.

Here we are beginning to deal with considerations of a sort that we must not simplify in our polemical enthusiasm. The writer publishes. To publish is to make public; but to make public is not just to bring about a simple displacement, causing something to pass from the private state to the public state, as though from one place—the innermost heart, the closed room—to another place—the outside, the street. Nor is it a matter of revealing a piece of news or a secret to one person in particular. The "public" is not made up of a large or small number of readers, each reading for himself. Writers like to say that they write their books intending them for a single friend. A resolution that is certain to be disappointed. There is no place in the public for a friend. There is no place for a particular person; any more than there is for particular social structures—families, groups, classes, nations. No one is part of the public and yet the whole world belongs to it, and not only the human world but all worlds, all things and no thing: the others. Because of this, no matter what severe censorship is imposed, no matter how faithfully the orders are obeyed, for authority there is always something suspect and displeasing about the act of publishing. This is because it causes the public to exist, and the public, always indeterminate, eludes the firmest political determinations.

To publish is not to cause oneself to be read, and it is not to give anything to be read. What is public is precisely what does not need to be read; it is always known already, in advance, with a kind of knowledge that knows everything and does not want to know anything. The public's interest, which is always excited, insatiable, and yet satisfied, which finds everything interesting but at the same time takes no interest in anything, is a movement that has been very wrongly described in a disparaging way. Here we see the same impersonal power, though in a relaxed and stabilized form, that lies at the origin of the literary effort as both obstacle and resource. The author speaks against an undefined and incessant speech, a speech without beginning or end—against it but also with its help. The reader eventually reads against the public's interest, against that distracted, unstable, versatile and omniscient curiosity, and he emerges with difficulty from that first reading which has already read before it reads: reading against it but even so through it. The reader, participating in a neutral kind of understanding, and the author, participating in a neutral kind of speech, would like to suspend these for a moment to allow room for a clearer form of expression.

Take the institution of literary prizes. It is easily explained by the structure of modern publishing and the social and economic organization of intellectual life. But when we think about the satisfaction that a writer, with rare exceptions, inevitably feels as he receives a prize that often represents nothing, we must explain it not in terms of the fact that his vanity has been flattered, but of his strong need for that communication before communication which is public understanding, in terms of the appeal of the profound and superficial clamor, in which everything appears, disappears, but remains, within a vague presence, a sort of River Styx that flows in broad daylight through our streets and irresistibly draws the living as though they were already shades, eager to become memorable so as to be better forgotten.

Nor is it a question of influence. It is not even a question of the pleasure of being seen by the blind crowd, or of being known by unknown people, a pleasure that implies the transformation of an indeterminate presence into a specific public, already defined, that is, the degeneration of an impalpable movement into a perfectly manipulable and accessible reality. On a slightly lower level, we will find all the political frivolities of the spectacle. But the writer will never win at this game. The most famous writer is not as well known as a daily radio announcer. And if he is eager to have intellectual power, he knows that he is wasting it in this insignificant notoriety. I believe the writer does not want anything for himself or for his work. But the need to be published—that is, to achieve outside existence, to attain that opening onto the outside, that divulgence-dissolution that takes place in our large cities—belongs to the work, like the memory of the impulse it grew out of, an impulse it must keep prolonging even though it wants to overcome it absolutely, an impulse it terminates for an instant, in effect, every time it is a work.

This reign of the "public," by which we mean the "outside" (the attractive force of a presence that is always there—not close, not distant, not familiar, not strange, it has no center, it is a kind of space that assimilates everything and retains nothing) has changed the writer's destination. Just as he has become a stranger to glory, just as he prefers anonymous groping to renown, and has lost all desire for immortality, so is he gradually—although at first glance this may seem less certain—abandoning the kind of pursuit of power that Barrès on the one hand and Monsieur Teste on the other—one by exerting an influence and the other by refusing to exert that influence—incarnated as two very characteristic types. You will say: "But never before have people who write been so involved in politics. Look at the petitions they sign, the interest they show, look how readily they believe they are authorized to judge everything simply because they write." It is true: when two writers meet, they never talk about literature (fortunately); their first remarks are always about politics. I want to suggest that in general writers are quite without any desire to play a role or assert power or hold a magistracy, rather, they are surprisingly modest even in their fame, and very far removed from the cult of personality (actually, this trait is a consistent way to distinguish which of two contemporary writers is a modern writer and which an old-fashioned writer); the fact is that they are the more drawn to politics the more they stand shivering in the outside, at the edge of the public's uneasiness, seeking that communication before communication whose attraction they feel constantly invited to respect.

This can have the worst kind of result. It produces "these omniscient *observers*, these omniscient *chatterboxes*, these omniscient *pedants*, who know everything about everything and settle everything right away, who are quick to make final judgments about things that have just happened, so that soon it will be impossible for us to learn anything: we already know everything," whom Dionys Mascolo describes in his essay "on France's intellectual poverty."[1] Mascolo adds: "People here are informed, intelligent and acquisitive. They understand everything. They understand each thing so quickly that they do not take the time to think about anything. They do not understand anything . . . Just try forcing people who have already understood everything to admit that something *new* has happened!" Exactly these characteristics—though in this description they are slightly exaggerated and pointed, even

---

[1] Dionys Mascolo, *Lettre polonaise sur la misère intellectuelle en France* (*Polish Letter on France's Intellectual Poverty*).

degenerative—belong to public existence: neutral comprehension, infinite opening, intuitive and presentient understanding in which everyone is always up to date on recent events and has already decided about everything, meanwhile ruining every true value judgment. And so this apparently has the worst sort of result. But it also creates a new kind of situation in which the writer, in some sense losing his own existence and his individual certainty, and experiencing a kind of communication that is still indeterminate and as powerful as it is impotent, as full as it is empty, sees himself, as Mascolo remarks so justly, "reduced to impotence," "but reduced also to simplicity."

We might say that when the writer becomes involved in politics today, with an energy the experts do not like, he is still not involved in politics but rather in the new, scarcely perceived relationship that the literary work and literary language are seeking to arouse through contact with the public presence. This is why, when he talks about politics, he is already talking about something else—ethics; and talking about ethics, he is talking about ontology; talking about ontology, he is talking about poetry; when he talks, finally, about literature, "his only passion," it is only to revert to politics, "his only passion." This mobility is deceptive and can, once again, result in the worst kind of thing: those futile discussions that publicly active men unfailingly call "byzantine" or "intellectual" (qualifiers that are themselves, naturally, a part of that empty loquaciousness, when they do not serve to hide the irritable weakness of powerful men). All we can say about such mobility—whose difficulties and facilities, whose requirements and risks, have been shown us by Surrealism, which Mascolo correctly describes and defines²—is that it is never mobile enough, never faithful enough to that anguishing and extremely fatiguing instability that keeps growing and cultivates in all speech the refusal to abide by any definitive statement.

---

² "I must emphasize the extreme importance of Surrealism, the only intellectual movement in France in the first half of the twentieth century . . . . With a rigorousness that can in no way be called outmoded, Surrealism alone, between the two World Wars, was able to issue demands that were at once the demands of pure thought and the direct demands of men. Only Surrealism, with untiring tenacity, was able to recall that *revolution and poetry are the same thing."*

I must add that even though, because of this mobility, the writer is dissuaded from being any kind of expert, incapable even of being an expert in literature, much less in a particular literary genre, he nevertheless does not strive for the universality which the *honnête homme* of the seventeenth century, then Goethean man, and finally man in the classless society—not to speak of man in the conception of Father Teilhard, who is yet further removed—propose to us as a fantasy and a goal. Just as public understanding has always understood everything already, in advance, but obstructs all true understanding; just as the public clamor is absence and void of all firm and decided speech, always saying something other than what is said (producing a perpetual and formidable mix-up that Ionesco allows us to laugh at); just as the public is indetermination that destroys every group and every class; so the writer, coming under the fascination of what is at stake when he "publishes," and, seeking a reader in the public as Orpheus did Eurydice in Hell, turns to a kind of speech that is the speech of no one and that no one will understand, because it is always addressed to someone else, always awakening another person in the person who hears it, always arousing the expectation of something different. This speech is not universal, not something that would make literature a Promethean or divine power, having rights over everything, but rather the movement of a speech that is dispossessed and rootless, that prefers to say nothing rather than to claim to say everything, and each time it says something, only designates the level beneath which one must still descend if one wants to begin speaking. In our "intellectual poverty," then, there is also the wealth of thought, there is the indigence that gives us the presentiment that to think is always to learn to think less than we think, to think the absence which is also thought, and when we speak, to preserve this absence by bringing it to speech, if only—as is happening today— through an excess of repetitions and prolixity.

Nevertheless, when a writer rushes so eagerly into a concern for the anonymous and neutral existence that is public existence, when he seems to have no other interest, no other horizon, isn't he becoming involved in something that should never occupy him, or at least only indirectly? When Orpheus descends into hell in search of the work, he confronts a completely different Styx: a nocturnal separation that he must enchant with a look, but a look that does not freeze it. This is the essential experience, the only experience in which he must engage himself completely. Once he has returned to daylight, his only role in relation to the exterior powers is to disappear, quickly torn to pieces by their delegates, the Maenads, while the diurnal Styx, the river of public clamor in which his body has been scattered, carries within itself the work, singing, and not only carries it but wants to transform itself into song within it, maintain in the work its own fluid reality, its infinitely murmuring flux, stranger to all shores.

If the writer today, thinking he is descending into Hell, is satisfied with descending as far as the street, this is because the two rivers, the two great movements of primary communication, flow into one another and tend to mingle. This is because the profound primordial clamor—in which something is said but without speech, or something is silent but without silence—is not unlike the speech that does not speak, the understanding that is misunderstood and always listening, that is the public "mind" and "way." The result of this is that very often the work seeks to be published before it exists, it seeks its realization not in the space that is its own but through exterior animation, that life which appears sumptuous but which is dangerously inconsistent as soon as one tries to appropriate it.

Such confusion is not accidental. This extraordinary muddle, which results in the writer publishing before he has written, the public forming and transmitting what it does not understand, the critic judging and defining what he does not read, and lastly the reader being forced to read what has not yet been written—this movement, which confuses all the different moments in the formation of the work by anticipating them each time, also brings them together in a quest for a new unity. Whence the richness and the poverty, the pride and the humility, the extreme disclosure and the extreme solitude of our literary effort, which at least has the merit of desiring neither power nor glory.

Wittgenstein's Problem

Flaubert.

There is no question that Flaubert marks an epoch in the history of writing, if we assume that the pursuit of *the act of writing* —that silent, absent, and perverse demon which makes every writer of the modern age a Faust without magic—can take the shape of history.

And yet almost every time he expresses his theoretical preoccupations —exalting Art, asserting Form or else exhausting himself through Work—we are at once fascinated and disappointed by what he says: as though something else were active within what he was trying to say, something more essential, though unformulated, tormenting and attracting him. This is why he always felt that his correspondents misunderstood him, why he had to repeat himself and contradict himself to the point where in the end the only thing that emerged was the excessiveness of an absurd passion or the irritability of a labor at loose ends. For example, he glorifies prose; this is one of his important discoveries. He says that prose is more difficult than poetry, that it is the summit of art, that French prose could attain an inconceivable beauty. But what does he mean by prose? Not just the space of the novel (which was for the first time, even after Balzac, raised to some kind of absolute existence), but the enigma of language as it is written, the paradox of direct speech (*prorsa oratio*), bent by the essential detour, the perversion of writing. It is the same with form: he wants beautiful form, he wants to write *well*, he hunts down repetitions and discordances in his sentences, he believes that exact prose should speak very loudly. An ideal we have moved far away from. Then all of a sudden he corrects himself: form is nothing but idea—and here he understands it in the classical sense, as a student of Boileau; write well in order to think well;[1] form and substance insepara-

---

[1] *"One never lacks for the word when one possesses the idea."*

ble, even indistinguishable; then, once more, he reverses the requirements: "I try to think well *in order to* write well. But my aim is to write
well, I don't deny it." And what does it mean to write well? When
George Sand reproaches him for his obvious inclination to beautiful,
sonorous, well-rounded sentences, he immediately answers: "The
rounding of a sentence is nothing, but to write *well* is everything"—and
yet again, he reintroduces equivocation with this explanation borrowed
from Buffon: "To write well is at once to feel well, think well and speak
well" (let us point out that writing is conceived as a totality of which
expression is only one moment or one component, perhaps a secondary
determination). Finally, as almost always happens, the temptation of
capital letters leads him to a true Platonism in which salvation through
Form opens up a new heaven to him: "Fact is distilled in Form and rises
up as a pure incense of the Spirit towards the Eternal, the Immutable,
the Absolute, the Ideal."

As a purely plastic manifestation, intended to make the sentence a
beautiful visible and audible thing—the phrased, or beyond that, a
dependable way of mastering the formlessness that always threatens
it—Art, reduced to its formal values, oriented toward euphony alone,
seems to us quite alien to that power which Mallarmé will search for and
which, in relation to ordinary language, will be designated another
language, purer but also more unobtrusive, capable of calling into
question—in order to disappear in it—the very Other of all language,
this Other which, however, is nothing more than a language which also
has an Other in which it has to disappear—and so on indefinitely. In this
respect, then, we are tempted to say that Flaubert is not yet Mallarmé,
and as we read the collection of texts taken from his correspondence,[2] we
are tempted to recognize how difficult it is for a writer, even though he
may be very conscious of himself and of what is at stake in his task, to
perceive the experience he is struggling with as long as he tries to
understand that experience by referring to notions that are still perverted
by tradition and obscured by the state of society.

[2] A collection that Geneviève Bollème has carefully selected and entitled *Préface à la Vie
d'Ecrivain* (*Preface to a Writer's Life*) (Editions du Seuil)—a preface, it must be said, that
consumes the life itself.

For us everything is clear, almost too clear, in the process that is described to us this way in uncertain words. We hasten to reinterpret this confused past using the intelligence of the future, and as we distinguish, in the Hegelian manner, between the writer's experience as it was for him and that same experience as it is presented to us, it becomes apparent to us that it is Literature itself, in its capital truth, that progresses this way, detaches itself and deploys itself or even closes itself around its center, a center which is ever more interior, more hidden, and more absent. But is this really how it is? Aren't we laboring under an illusion? Aren't we reading as readable what has not even been written yet? Aren't we forgetting that although Flaubert was certainly at a turning point, we too are exposed to the demands of a "turning point," that movement of turning by turning away, for which we do not yet have sufficient theoretical methods of elucidation, sometimes apprehending it as the movement of historical development, sometimes becoming aware of it in terms of structures and recognizing it to be the enigma of every relationship, that is to say, in the end, of every language?

◆

It is the anguish of form that is important in Flaubert and not the signification that he gives it here and there—or, to put it more exactly, this anxiety is infinite, proportionate to the experience in which he feels he is engaged, and it has only very uncertain reference points to define its direction. The engagement of the writer Flaubert is an engagement—a responsibility—to a still unknown language that he makes an effort to hasten or subject to some kind of reason (that of a value, beauty, truth), the better to sense the hazardous power which what is unknown in this language forces him to confront. He is not at all ignorant of it: he specifically says that for him the search for form is a method ("the concern for external beauty with which you reproach me is for me a *method*"); which certainly means that form has the value of a Law that is posed arbitrarily but that responds to what is arbitrary—the indeterminate—in all speech, that is, to its essentially problematical trait.

The more sumptuous, splendid, dazzling art is, the more it manifests itself in solely exterior artifices, and also the more it will seek—as its too

glorious appearance exposes the emptiness hidden within it—to unite
with its own obliteration—an impulse Flaubert certainly does not act on
intentionally but whose ruinous meaning was revealed in his last book:
the question no longer being to know whether B. and P. are "imbeciles
through and through" or, quite the opposite, perfectly human individuals, at once mediocre and sublime, dedicated to exertion and failure,
predecessors of Bloom and successors of Ulysses, but rather how nullity
becomes a work and how the totality of an encyclopedic knowledge
(therefore a maximum of substance) can coincide on the level of literature with the nothingness without which Flaubert suspects that there is
no literary affirmation. (In this way, *Bouvard et Pécuchet* paradoxically
fulfills the desire of the young Flaubert: *"What seems beautiful to me,
what I would like to make, would be a book about nothing, a book
without any exterior attachment . . . "*) After having demanded that
style be governed by the law of numbers, that it be agreeable to the ear
because of its so-called musical qualities (understood in a completely
exterior sense), he also knows very well, as though in spite of himself,
that "Art must be a good fellow," not let itself be seen, give up everything
pleasurable, confine itself within the austerity of nonappearance, where
"the unwitting poetics" rules—a revealing formulation. The same goes
for working. No writer has worked harder than he did, or done more to
reduce the condition of people who write to that of the "horrible work-
ers." Listening to him and watching him toil away, we feel as though a
book is made in the same way a beautiful object used to be made in the
old days: with care, with skill, and in one single stretch of time. But at
the same time, it is immediately apparent that Flaubert's work has
nothing in common with Boileau's: this is not the honest and tranquil
work of a craftsman who has a trade and a certain technical knowledge,
who brings the work to perfection by conforming to a tradition and on
the basis of a model. Here, during the very period when work becomes
the sign for every value, it is without value and in fact tragic;[3] it is
something excessive; it is a kind of madness; it is an encounter with the

---

[3] It is as though Flaubert were trying to use the plus-value available in work (once the
writer, the editor, the critic, the reader, and the finished work all become owners of it),
to compensate for and overcome the strange minus-value that the more one speaks the
less one speaks.

terrifying, a confrontation with the inhuman, the practice of the impossible, the initiation of a torture. And one works in order to make what? A work of literature that does not exist, a beautiful unreal book? Not even that: a sentence, and a sentence that cannot be written: "The simplest sentence, like 'he shut the door,' 'he went out,' requires incredible artistic ruses"; which no doubt means that the most ordinary actions are very difficult to formulate, but that in a deeper sense, on the level of literature, the sentence "he closed the door" is, as such, already impossible.

This is the source of all the statements that people have found laughable or merely pathetic, until they begin to take them seriously: "I have arrived at the conviction that it is *impossible to write*" (and the italics are Flaubert's). "Writing is more and more impossible," and because of this "despair is [his] normal state," he can emerge from it only by means of some violent distraction, exhausting himself, "panting without relief" in that exercise of writing that exceeds life, because writing is that excess itself ("Art exceeds"). Then why persist in this unhappiness, why not rest from it? "But how can I rest? And what should I do while I am resting?" "There is a mystery here that escapes me," a mystery, however, that he helps us to approach when he writes the following to one of his correspondents—and it must be understood without reservation: "*This is what is diabolical about prose, that it is never finished.*" Because of this, all the works he undertakes are extravagant; in each one, he is shattered by "horrifying" difficulties; each time he promises himself that the next one will be easy, happy, more suited to his talent, and each time he chooses the only one he cannot write: "I must be absolutely mad to undertake a book like this one . . . I must be crazy and completely out of my mind to undertake such a book! I am afraid that in its very conception it is radically impossible . . . What terror! I feel as though I'm about to embark on a very long voyage towards unknown regions, and that I won't be coming back." Which is the reason for the dry and dark conclusion with which, five years before he died, he began his patient and malicious wait for death: "I don't expect anything more from life than a succession of sheets of paper to be scribbled on in black. I feel I am crossing an endless solitude, going I know not where. And I am at once the desert, the traveler, and the camel." (To George Sand, March

27, 1875, after having noted: "Perhaps it is the work that is making me ill, because I have undertaken an extravagant book.")

◆

The fact that Flaubert was attracted by the search for a new meaning to give the word "writing" is clear from reading this note: "I would like to make books in which it would only be a matter of *writing* sentences . . ." In underlining the word writing, Flaubert was not trying to emphasize it but to make it appear; he was trying to indicate that this verb is not used up by its transitive power and that the work proper to it is a work of intransitivity. The book and the sentences are only modes of what is at stake when one writes. One writes, and one writes (sentences); but the result remains between parentheses; this result—sentences, a book—does not even serve to give validity to "writing" or to define its proper value or transform it into a value (the way, for example, the Creation gave validity to God as a creative power). One writes sentences so that the visibility of the sentence will cover over and preserve the privilege of invisibility and the power of disclaiming and effacement that do not allow "writing" to be anything else but a neuter word.

Roussel.

When Michel Foucault, pondering Raymond Roussel, defines as a meeting ground for madness and the work the central void Artaud bore witness to with his screams[4]—we inevitably think of the accusatory formulation that Flaubert used exactly one hundred years ago to communicate to Louise Collet his difficulties: *"I know very well that the creative art of style is not as large as the entire idea. But whose fault is*

---

[4] *"This solar hollow . . . is the space of Roussel's language, the void he speaks from, the absence through which the work and madness communicate and exclude one another. And I don't mean this void metaphorically: it is a matter of the insufficiency of words that are less numerous than the things they designate, and owe to this economy the fact that they mean something."* Farther along, Michel Foucault alludes to *"an experience that surfaces in our times, teaching us that what is lacking is not 'meaning,' but the signs that nevertheless only signify through this lack."* (*Raymond Roussel*, "Le Chemin" collection, Gallimard.)

that? The fault of the language. We have too many things and not enough forms. That is what tortures the conscientious person . . . " A striking coincidence. But what is really striking is not the coincidence, it is the long distance that literary activity has had to travel from one of these coinciding reflections to the other. Flaubert clearly sees the truth of the language in this "too many things" and this "not enough forms," though he does not hasten to rejoice over it, and he regards this defect as the writer's reason for existing, since the writer is called upon to make up for it through labor, skill, and cunning. "Too many things," "not enough forms"—a poverty he deplores, since it obliges him to give only limited expression to so much wealth. This corresponds to Lévi-Strauss's hypothesis: that art is essentially reduction, the creation of a reduced model. Except that, far from feeling distressed by this, Lévi-Strauss cheerfully describes to us all the advantages of the reductive power of both the plastic arts and—this is implied—of language. ("Being smaller, the totality of the object seems less formidable; because it is quantitatively diminished, it seems to us quantitatively simplified; this quantitative transposition increases and diversifies our power over a homologue of the thing.")

But let us think about this. I wonder if Flaubert's uneasiness is not justified—on the condition, however, that we turn his formula around, saying: "Always too many forms," that is, that there is always too much of what we never have enough of. The problem, as we sense, is that the inadequacy of language—once we recognize it as the essence of speaking—runs the risk of never being sufficiently inadequate. Lack of language: what this means (to begin with) is two things—a lack with respect to what has to be signified, but at the same time a lack that is the center and the life of meaning, the reality of speech (and the relationship between these two lacks is itself incommensurable). To speak—as we know today—is to bring this kind of lack into play, maintain it and deepen it in order to make it *be* more and more, and in the end what it puts in our mouths and under our hands is no longer the pure absence of signs but the prolixity of an indefinitely and indifferently signifying absence: a designation that remains impossible to annul, even if it carries nullity within it. If it were not this way, we would all have been satisfied with silence long ago. But this very silence—the lack of signs—

itself remains always significant and always excessive in relation to the ambiguous lack involved in speech.

Let us think about it a little more. "Too many things" is the Other of language, which is itself, then, regarded as "forms," the latter being assumed to be merely finite in number (as Flaubert and Lévi-Strauss postulate), while things would correspond to some kind of infinity (or indefiniteness). But the characteristic of a form of language is that it only contains something as long as it contains nothing. Which amounts to concluding that if there are "not enough forms," this is true only for a language that considers form to be already and merely a thing. In other words, even if there is only a finite number of structures, that is, a determined number of kinds of relations, as long as just one of them is such that it expresses (holds) the infinite, Flaubert's statement can be turned around, and one should not complain about "too many things" but rather "never enough things," the entire universe, then, being not enough to fill the Danaids' barrel.

Finally, and to move ahead more quickly: the problem defined by Flaubert is the question of the *Other* of speech. Now, ever since Mallarmé we have felt that the other of language is always posed by the language itself as that in which it looks for a way out, in order to disappear into it, or for an Outside, in which to be reflected. Which means not simply that the Other is already part of *this* language, but that as soon as this language turns around to respond to its Other, it is turning towards another language, and we must be aware that this other language is other, and also that it, too, has its Other. At this point we come very close to Wittgenstein's problem, as corrected by Bertrand Russell: that every language has a structure about which one can say nothing *in* that language, but that there must be another language dealing with the structure of the first and possessing a new structure about which one cannot say anything except in a third language—and so forth. Several consequences follow from this, among them these: 1) what is inexpressible is inexpressible in relation to a certain system of expression; 2) although there may be reason to regard the group of things and values as constituting a whole (for example, in a given scientific conception, perhaps a certain given political one), the virtual group of the different possibilities of speech could not constitute a totality; 3) the Other of all speech is never anything but the Other of a given speech or else the *infinite movement* through which one mode of expression—always prepared to extend itself in the multiple requirements of simultaneous series—fights itself, exalts itself, challenges itself or obliterates itself in some other mode.[5]

◆

Bearing these remarks in mind, I would like to return to the work of Roussel, restored to us in its speaking presence by Michel Foucault's book. Yes, if we bear these remarks in mind, it seems to me that we will become more fully aware of the prodigious effect it produces on us (independent of its actual inventions), to the extent that the work, through its passage from a description to an explanation, and then, within the explanation, to a tale that, though hardly begun, opens to give rise to a new enigma that must in its turn be described, then in its turn be explained, something that cannot be done without the enigma of a new tale—through this series of intervals perpetually opening out from one another, the work of Roussel represents, in a coldly concerted and particularly dizzying manner, the infinite navigation from one sort of language to another sort, in which the affirmation of that *Other* keeps appearing for an instant in profile and disappearing, that Other which is no longer the inexpressible depth but the play of the manoeuvers or mechanisms destined to avert it; this is why descriptions, explanations, talks, commentaries function as if of their own accord, flatly, mechanically, in order to channel the void or the lack through a system of openings and closings that this lack alone sets in motion and keeps in motion. We can only record —with rather fearful surprise—that in this respect there is a kinship between *Locus Solus*, *L'Etoile au Front*, and

---

[5] When Flaubert says, with naivety and malice, "Too many things," "not enough forms," he is not contrasting a richness—the richness of the unsayable real—to a poverty—the poverty of words that are too few and too awkward to say it; although he does not know it, all he is doing is contrasting one language with another: one is fixed to the level of its content and is semantically full, the other is reduced to its formal values and fixed in its pure signifying decision—this is an opposition he cannot affirm in either of these two languages, but using a third, and speaking from higher up, he pronounces his judgment: "Too many things," "not enough forms."

his early works, constructed around a play of parentheses. Inevitably we would then be tempted to ascribe the obsession of this process to the perversity of some kind of madness, and there is nothing scandalous about that; but since madness itself—whatever sort it may be—is only a language of a particular kind that we will try our best, if we are knowledgeable, to transpose into another language, as we do this, no matter how careful we are, we will simply be embarking in our own turn, *as blind people,* on this navigation that does not end in either a harbor or a shipwreck: we will all be committed, with more or less pomposity or simplicity, to the game of displacement without place, reduplication without duplication, reiteration without repetition—these proceedings that roll up and unroll inside one another infinitely and without moving, as if in this way the word that is too many could be used up.[6]

---

[6] Wittgenstein, Flaubert, Roussel say the following: if there were a certain discourse—scientific, for example—such that lack could not find a place there in which to inscribe itself so as to act as effect, the lack would nevertheless *already* be inscribed there, if only because of the need or the demand for *another* language invoked to determine the meaning, the theoretical possibility of this discourse without lack. If a language owes its perpetual failure to this lack, the lack in turn has an obligation to the language to attain within it—through an infinite passage from one mode of saying to another, even if it was not marked in that region of discourse— to attain within that language (scattering there, at that moment, in the moving plurality of a place that is always unoccupied) at the limit, an excess of place—"the word that is too many." It is perhaps this "word that is too many" that constitutes (while immediately dismissing him) the invisible partner, the one that does not play, and it is in relation to this invisible partner that Roger Laporte's books continue to be written.

The Narrative Voice
(the "he," the neuter)

I write (I pronounce) this sentence: "The life forces are sufficient only up to a certain point." As I pronounce it, I have something very simple in mind: the sensation of weariness that constantly makes us feel that life is limited; you take a few steps down the street, eight or nine, then you fall. The limit set by weariness limits life. The meaning of life is in turn limited by this limit: a limited meaning of a limited life. But a reversal occurs, a reversal that can be discovered in various different ways. Language alters the situation. The sentence I pronounce tends to draw into the very inside of life the limit that was only supposed to mark it on the outside. Life is called limited. The limit does not disappear, but it takes from language the perhaps not unlimited meaning that it claims to limit: the meaning of the limit, by affirming it, contradicts the limitation of meaning or at least displaces it; but because of this there is a risk of losing the knowledge of the limit understood as limitation of meaning. Then how are we to speak of this limit (convey its meaning), without allowing the meaning to un-limit it? Here, we must enter another kind of language, and in the meantime realize that the sentence "The life forces . . . " is not, as such, entirely possible.

◆

Nevertheless, let us adhere to it. Let us write a tale in which it has a place as an achievement of the tale itself. What is the difference between these two identical sentences? There is certainly a very great difference. I can describe it roughly this way: the tale is like a circle that neutralizes life, which is not to say that it has no relationship to it but that its relationship to it is a neutral one. Within this circle, the meaning of what is, and of what is said, is definitely still given, but from a withdrawn position, from a distance where all meaning and all lack of meaning is neutralized beforehand. A reserve that exceeds every meaning already signified, without being considered a richness or a pure and simple privation. It is like speech that does not illuminate and does not obscure.

Often, in a bad tale—assuming that there are bad tales, which is not altogether certain—we have the impression that someone is speaking in the background and prompting the characters or even the events with what they have to say: an indiscreet and clumsy intrusion; it is said to be the author talking, an authoritarian and complacent "I" still anchored in life and barging in without any restraint. It is true, this is indiscreet— and this is how the circle is wiped out. But it is also true that the impression that someone is talking "in the background" is really part of the singularity of narrative and the truth of the circle: as though the center of the circle lay outside the circle, in back and infinitely far back, as though the *outside* were precisely this center, which could only be the absence of all center. Now, isn't this outside, this "in back"—which is in no way a dominating or lofty space from which one could grasp every- thing in a single glance and command the events (of the circle)—isn't this the very distance that language receives, as its limit, from its own deficiency, a distance that is certainly altogether exterior, but that inhabits language and in some sense constitutes it, an infinite distance such that to stay within language is always to be already outside, a distance such that, if it were possible to accept it, to "relate" it in the sense appropriate to it, one could then speak of the limit, that is, bring to the point of speech an experience of limits and the limit-experience? Regarded from this point of view, then, the tale is the hazardous space where the sentence "The life forces . . . " can be asserted in its truth, but where, in turn, all sentences, even the most innocent ones, risk assuming the same ambiguous status that language assumes at its limit. A limit that is perhaps the neuter.

◆

I will not hark back to the subject of "the use of personal pronouns in the novel," which has given rise to so many noteworthy studies.[1] I think

---

[1] I am referring to Michel Butor's *Répertoire II* (Éditions de Minuit).

I should go farther back. If, as has been shown (in *L'Espace littéraire*), to write is to pass from "I" to "he," but if "he" when substituted for "I" does not simply designate another me, any more than it does esthetic disinterestedness—that impure contemplative enjoyment that allows the reader and the spectator to participate in the tragedy as a distraction—what remains to be discovered is what is at stake when writing responds to the demands of this uncharacterizable "he." In the narrative form, we hear—and always as though in addition to other things—something indeterminate speaking, something that the evolution of this form outlines, isolates, so that it gradually becomes manifest, though in a deceptive way. The "he" is the unlighted occurrence of what takes place when one tells a story. The distant epic narrator recounts exploits that happened and that he seems to be reproducing, whether or not he witnessed them. But the narrator is not a historian. His song is the domain where the event that takes place there comes to speech, in the presence of a memory; memory—muse and mother of muses—contains within it truth, that is, the reality of what takes place; it is in his song that Orpheus really descends to the underworld—which we express by adding that he descends to it through the power of his singing; but this song, already instrumental, signifies an alteration in the institution of narration. To tell a story is a mysterious thing. The mysterious "he" of the epic institution very quickly divides: the "he" becomes the impersonal coherence of a *story* (in the full and rather magical meaning of this word); the *story* stands by itself, preformed in the thought of a demiurge, and since it exists on its own, there is nothing left to do but tell it. But the *story* soon becomes disenchanted. The experience of the disenchanted world introduced into literature by Don Quixote is the experience that dissipates the *story* by contrasting it to the banality of the real—this is how realism seizes on the form of the novel, for a long time to come, and this form becomes the most effective genre for the developing bourgeoisie. The "he" is here uneventful everyday life, what happens when nothing happens, the course of the world as it is unnoticed, the passing of time, routine and monotonous life. At the same time—and in a more visible way—the "he" marks the intrusion of a character: the novelist is a person who refuses to say "I" but delegates that power to other people; the novel is filled with little "egos"—

tormented, ambitious, unhappy, though always satisfied in their unhappiness; the individual asserts himself in his subjective richness, his inner freedom, his psychology; the novelistic narration, that of individuality—not taking into consideration the content itself—is already marked by an ideology to the extent that it assumes that the individual, with all his particular characteristics and his limits, is enough to express the world, that is to say, it assumes that the course of the world remains that of the individual.

As we can see, then, the "he" has split in two: on the one hand, there is something to tell, and that is the *objective* reality as it is immediately present to the interested gaze, and on the other hand, this reality is reduced to a constellation of individual lives, *subjectivities*, a multiple and personalized "he," a manifest "ego" under the veil of an apparent "he." In the interval of the tale, the voice of the narrator can be heard with more or less appropriateness, sometimes fictive, sometimes without any mask.

What has surrendered in this remarkable construction? Almost everything. I will not dwell on it.

◆

There is something else that should be said. Let us draw a comparison—while remaining aware of the clumsiness of such a procedure, since it is unduly simplistic—between the impersonality of the novel as it is rightly or wrongly attributed to Flaubert and the impersonality of a novel by Kafka. The impersonality of the impersonal novel is the impersonality of esthetic distance. The rule is imperious: the novelist must not intervene. The author—even if *Madame Bovary* is *myself*—does away with all direct relations between himself and the novel; reflection, commentary, moralizing intrusion, still brilliantly legitimate in Stendhal or Balzac, become mortal sins. Why? For two reasons that are different but that almost merge. The first: what is told has an esthetic value to the extent that the interest one takes in it is interest from a distance; disinterestedness—an essential category in the judgment of taste since Kant and even since Aristotle—means that an esthetic act should not be based on an interest, if it wants to create a legitimate interest. A disinterested interest. Thus the author must heroically move away and keep his distance so that the reader or the spectator can also remain at a distance. The ideal is still the performance of classical theater: the narrator is there only to raise the curtain; the play is really performed from time immemorial and in some sense without him; he does not tell—he shows; and the reader does not read—he looks, attending, taking part without participating. The other reason is almost the same, though it is completely different: the author must not intervene, because the novel is a work of art and the work of art exists all by itself, an unreal thing, in the world outside the world, it must be left free, the props must be removed, the moorings cut, so that it can be sustained in its status as an imaginary object (but here Mallarmé, that is, an entirely different requirement, is already on the horizon).

Let us talk about Thomas Mann for a moment. His is an interesting case, because he does not respect the rule of nonintervention: he constantly involves himself in what he is telling, sometimes through interposed persons, but also in the most direct kind of way. What about this unwarranted intrusion? It is not moralizing—a stand taken against a certain character—it does not consist of illuminating things from outside—the thrust of the creator's thumb as he shapes his figures the way he wants them. It represents the intervention of the narrator challenging the very possibility of narration—an intervention that is, consequently, an essentially critical one, but in the manner of a game, of a malicious irony. Flaubert's kind of impersonality, contracted and difficult, still affirmed the validity of the narrative mode: to tell was to show, to allow to be or to make exist, without there being any reason—despite the great doubts one could already entertain—to question oneself about the limits and the shapes of the narrative form. Thomas Mann knows very well that we have lost our naivety. He therefore tries to restore it, not by ignoring illusion, but on the contrary, by creating it, making it so visible that he plays with it, just as he plays with the reader and by doing so draws him into the game. With his great sense of the narrative feast, Thomas Mann thus succeeds in restoring it as a feast of the narrative illusion, giving us back a second degree ingenuousness, that of the absence of ingenuousness. One could therefore say that if esthetic distance is denounced in his work, it is also proclaimed, affirmed by a narrative awareness that adopts itself as theme, whereas in the more traditional impersonal novel, it disappeared, putting itself between parentheses. Storytelling was a matter of course.

Storytelling is not a matter of course. As we know, the narrative act is generally taken in charge by a certain character, not that this character tells the story directly, or makes himself the narrator of a story that has already been experienced or that is in the process of being experienced, but because he constitutes the center around which the perspective of the tale is organized: everything is seen from this point of view. There is, therefore, a privileged "I," if only that of a character discussed in the third person, who takes great pains not to exceed the possibilities of his knowledge and the limits of his position: this is the realm of James's ambassadors, and it is also the realm of the subjectivist formulae, in which the authenticity of the narrative depends on the existence of a free subject—formulae that are correct insofar as they represent the decision to stick to a certain prejudice (obstinacy and even obsession constitute one of the rules that seem to be imposed when writing is involved—form is obstinate, that is its danger), correct but in no way definitive, because on the one hand they wrongly assert that there might be some kind of equivalency between the narrative act and the transparency of a consciousness (as though to tell were simply to be conscious, to project, to reveal, to cover up by revealing), and on the other hand they maintain the primacy of the individual consciousness, which they say is only secondly and even secondarily an articulate consciousness.

◆

In the meantime, Kafka wrote. Kafka admires Flaubert. The novels he writes are marked by an austerity that would permit a distracted reader to place them in the line of Flaubert. Yet everything is different. One of these differences is essential to the subject we are discussing. Distance—creative disinterestedness (so evident in Flaubert to the extent that he has to struggle to maintain it)—the distance that was the writer's and the reader's distance from the work and permitted the pleasure of contemplation, now enters into the very sphere of the work in the guise of an irreducible strangeness. No longer challenged, reestablished as something denounced, as in Thomas Mann (or Gide), it is the environment of the novelistic world, the space in which the narrative experience unfolds in unique simplicity—the experience one does not recount but that is involved when one recounts. A distance that is not simply lived as such by the central character, always at a distance from himself, just as he is at a distance from the events he experiences or the people he encounters (that would still be only the manifestation of a singular I); a distance that distances even him, removing him from the center, since it constantly decenters the work, in a way that is not measurable and not discernible, at the same time as it introduces into the most rigorous narration the alteration of another kind of speech or of the other as speech (as writing).

The consequences of this sort of change will often be misinterpreted. One consequence, immediately evident, is noteworthy. As soon as the alien distant becomes the stake and seems the substance of the story, the reader, who until then has been identifying, though from afar, with the story in progress (living it, for his part, in the mode of contemplative irresponsibility), can no longer be disinterested in it, that is, enjoy it with disinterestedness. What is happening? What new demand is being made on him? It is not that this concerns him: on the contrary, it does not concern him at all, and perhaps it does not concern anyone; it is in some way the *nonconcerning*, but in turn, the reader can no longer comfortably keep his distance from it, since there is no way that he can situate himself correctly in relation to what does not even present itself as unsituatable. Then how is he to remove himself from the absolute distance that has in some sense taken all removal back into itself? Without any support, deprived of the interest of reading, he is no longer allowed to look at things from far away, to keep that distance between them and himself that is the distance of the gaze, because the distant in its nonpresent presence, is not available either close up or far away and cannot be the object of a gaze. From now on, it is no longer a question of vision. Narration ceases to be what is presented to be seen, through a chosen actor-spectator as intermediary and from his viewpoint. The realm of the circumspect consciousness—of narrative circumspection (of the "I" that looks at everything around it and stands fast under its gaze)—has been subtly shaken, without of course coming to an end.

✦

What Kafka teaches us—even if this expression cannot be directly attributed to him—is that storytelling brings the neuter into play. Narration governed by the neuter is kept in the custody of the "he," the third person that is neither a third person, nor the simple cloak of impersonality. The "he" of narration in which the neuter speaks is not content to take the place usually occupied by the subject, whether the latter is a stated or implied "I" or whether it is the event as it takes place in its impersonal signification.[2] The narrative "he" dismisses all subjects, just as it removes every transitive action or every objective possibility. It does this in two forms: 1) the speech of the tale always lets us feel that what is being told is not being told by anyone: it speaks in the neuter; 2) in the neuter space of the tale, the bearers of speech, the subjects of the action—who used to take the place of characters—fall into a relationship of nonidentification with themselves: something happens to them, something they cannot recapture except by relinquishing their power to say "I" and what happens to them has always happened already: they can only account for it indirectly, as self-forgetfulness, the forgetfulness that introduces them into the present without memory that is the present of narrating speech.

Of course this does not mean that the tale necessarily relates a forgotten occurrence or the occurrence of the forgetfulness that dominates lives and societies which, separated from what they are—alienated, as we say—move as though in their sleep to try to recapture themselves. It is the tale—independently of its content—that is forgetfulness, so that to tell a story is to put oneself to the test of this first forgetfulness that precedes, initiates, and destroys all memory. In this sense, telling is the torment of language, the incessant search for its infinity. And the tale is

[2] The "he" does not simply take the place traditionally occupied by a subject; as a moving fragmentation, it changes what we mean by place: a fixed spot, unique or determined by its placement. Here we should say once again (confusedly): the "he," scattering after the fashion of a defect in the simultaneous plurality—the repetition—of a moving and diversely unoccupied place, designates "his" place as both the place from which he will always be lacking and which will thus remain empty, and also as a surplus of place, a place that is always too much: hypertopy.

nothing else but an allusion to the initial deviation that writing brings, that carries writing away and that causes us, as we write, to yield to a sort of perpetual turning away.

The act of writing—that deflected relationship to life through which what is of no concern is asserted.

The narrative "he," whether it is absent or present, whether it asserts itself or conceals itself, whether or not it changes the conventions of writing—linearity, continuity, readability—in this way marks the intrusion of the other—understood as neuter—in its irreducible strangeness, in its wily perversity. The other speaks. But when the other speaks, no one is speaking, because the other—which we must refrain from honoring with a capital letter that would establish it in a majestic substantive, as though it had some substantial, even unique, presence—is never precisely simply the other, rather it is neither one thing nor the other, and the neuter that indicates it withdraws it from both, as from the unity, always establishing it outside the term, the act, or the subject where it claims to exist. The narrative (I do not say narrating) voice derives its aphony from this. It is a voice that has no place in the work but does not hang over it either, far from falling out of some sky under the guarantee of a superior Transcendence: the "he" is not the "encompassing" of Jaspers, but rather a kind of void in the work—the absence-word that Marguerite Duras describes in one of her tales: "a hole-word, hollowed out in its center by a hole, by the hole in which all the other words should have been buried," and the text goes on: "One could not have spoken it, but one could have made it resound—immense, endless, an empty gong . . . "[3] It is the narrative voice, a neuter voice that speaks the work from that place-less place in which the work is silent.

◆

The narrative voice is neuter. Let us take a quick look at what traits characterize it at first approach. For one thing, it says nothing, not only because it adds nothing to what there is to say (it does not know any-

---

[3] *Le Ravissement de Lol V. Stein* (Gallimard) [*The Ravishing of Lol V. Stein*, trans. by Richard Seaver, Grove Press, 1966, p. 38]

thing), but because it underlies this nothing—the "to silence," and the "to keep silent"—in which speech is here and now already engaged; thus it is not heard, first of all, and everything that gives it a distinct reality begins to betray it. Then again, being without its own existence, speaking from nowhere, suspended in the tale as a whole, it is not dissipated there either, as light is, which, though invisible itself, makes things visible: it is radically exterior, it comes from exteriority itself, the outside that is the special enigma of language in writing. But let us consider still other traits, traits that are actually the same. The narrative voice that is inside only insofar as it is outside, at a distance without any distance, cannot be embodied: even though it can borrow the voice of a judiciously chosen character or even create the hybrid position of mediator (this voice which destroys all mediation), it is always different from what utters it, it is the indifferent-difference that alters the personal voice. Let us say (on a whim) that it is spectral, ghost-like. Not that it comes from beyond the grave and not even because it might represent once and for all some essential absence, but because it always tends to absent itself in its bearer and also to efface him as center, thus being neuter in the decisive sense that it cannot be central, does not create a center, does not speak from a center, but on the contrary, at the limit would prevent the work from having a center, withdrawing from it all special focus of interest, even that of afocality, and also not allowing it to exist as a completed whole, once and forever accomplished.

Tacit, it attracts language obliquely, indirectly and within this attraction—that of oblique speech—allows the neuter to speak. What does that indicate? The narrative voice carries the neuter. It carries the neuter in that: 1) to speak in the neuter is to speak at a distance, preserving that distance, without *mediation* or *community*, and even experiencing the infinite distancing of distance, its irreciprocity, its irrectitude or its asymmetry—because the greatest distance dominated by asymmetry, without one or another of its boundaries being privileged, is precisely the neuter (one cannot neutralize the neuter); 2) the neuter speech neither reveals nor conceals. This is not to say that it signifies nothing (by claiming to renounce sense in the form of nonsense), it means it does not signify in the same way the visible-invisible signifies, but that it opens another power in the language, one alien to the power of illumination (or of darkening), of comprehension (or of misapprehension). It does not signify in the optical manner; it remains outside the light-shadow reference that seems to be the ultimate reference of all knowledge and communication to the point of making us forget that it has only the value of a venerable, that is to say, inveterate, metaphor; 3) the demand of the neuter tends to suspend the attributive structure of the language, that relationship to being, implicit or explicit, that is immediately posed in our languages as soon as something is said. It has often been remarked—by philosophers, linguists, political commentators—that nothing can be denied that has not already been posed beforehand. To put it another way, all language begins by articulating, and in articulating it affirms. But it could be that telling (writing) is drawing language into a possibility of saying that would say without saying being and still without denying it either—or, more clearly, too clearly, that it is establishing the center of gravity of speech elsewhere, where speaking is not a matter of affirming being nor of needing negation in order to suspend the work of being, the work that ordinarily occurs in every form of expression. In this respect, the narrative voice is the most critical one that can communicate unheard. That is why we tend, as we listen to it, to confuse it with the oblique voice of unhappiness or the oblique voice of madness.[4]

[4] This voice—the narrative voice—is the one I hear, perhaps rashly, perhaps rightly, in the tale by Marguerite Duras that I mentioned a short while ago. The night forever without any dawn—that ballroom in which the indescribable event occurred that cannot be recalled and cannot be forgotten, but that one's forgetting retains—the nocturnal desire to turn around in order to see what belongs neither to the visible nor to the invisible, that is, to stay for a moment, through one's gaze, as close as possible to strangeness, where the rhythm of reveal-oneself-conceal-oneself has lost its guiding force—then, the need (the eternal human desire) to bring about acceptance in another person, to live once again in another person, a third person, the dual relationship, fascinated, indifferent, irreducible to any mediation: a neuter relationship, even if it implies the infinite void of desire—finally, the imminent certainty that what has happened once will always begin again, will always betray itself and reject itself: these really are, it seems to me, the "coordinates" of narrative space, that circle where, as we enter it, we incessantly enter the outside. But who is telling the story here? Not the reporter, the one who formally—and also a little shamefacedly—does the speaking, and actually takes over, so much so that he seems to us to be an intruder, but rather that which cannot tell a story because it bears—this is its wisdom, this is its madness—the torment of impossible narration, knowing (with a closed knowledge anterior to the reason-unreason split) that it is the measure of this outside, where, as we reach it, we are in danger of falling under the attraction of a completely exterior speech: pure extravagance.

The Absence of the Book

Let us try to question ourselves, that is, admit in the form of a question something that cannot reach the point of questioning.

1. *"This insane game of writing."* With these words, simple as they are, Mallarmé opens up writing to writing. The words are very simple, but their nature is also such that we will need a great deal of time—a great variety of experiments, the work of the world, countless misunderstandings, works lost and scattered, the movement of knowledge, and finally the turning point of an infinite crisis—if we are to begin to understand what decision is being prepared on the basis of this end of writing that is foretold by its coming.

2. Apparently we only read because the writing is already there, laid out before our eyes. Apparently. But the first person who ever wrote, who cut into stone and wood under ancient skies, was far from responding to the demands of a view that required a reference point and gave it meaning, changed all relations between seeing and the visible. What he left behind him was not something more, something added to other things; it was not even something less—a subtraction of matter, a hollow in the relation to the relief. Then what was it? A hole in the universe: nothing that was visible, nothing that was invisible. I suppose the first reader was engulfed by that non-absent absence, but without knowing anything about it, and there was no second reader because reading, from then on understood to be the vision of an immediately visible—that is, intelligible—presence, was affirmed for the very purpose of making this disappearance into *the absence of the book* impossible.

3. Culture is linked to the book. The book as repository and receptacle

of knowledge is identified with knowledge. The book is not only the book that sits in libraries—that labyrinth in which all combinations of forms, words and letters are rolled up in volumes. The book is the Book. Still to be read, still to be written, always already written, always already paralyzed by reading, the book constitutes the condition for every possibility of reading and writing.

The book admits of three distinct investigations. There is the empirical book; the book acts as vehicle of knowledge; a given determinate book receives and gathers a given determinate form of knowledge. But the book as book is never simply empirical. The book is the *a priori* of knowledge. We would know nothing if there did not always exist in advance the impersonal memory of the book and, more importantly, the prior inclination to write and read contained in every book and affirming itself only in the book. The absolute of the book, then, is the isolation of a possibility that claims not to have originated in any other anteriority. An absolute that will later tend to assert itself in the Romantics (Novalis), then more rigorously in Hegel, then more radically— though in a different way—in Mallarmé, as the totality of relations (absolute knowledge or the Work), in which would be achieved either consciousness, which knows itself and returns to itself after having been exteriorized in all its dialectically linked figures, or language, closed around its own statement and already dispersed.

Let us recapitulate: the empirical book; the book: condition for all reading and all writing; the book: totality or Work. But with increasing refinement and truth these forms all assume that the book contains knowledge as the presence of something virtually present and always immediately accessible, if only with the help of mediations and relays. Something is there which the book presents in presenting itself and which reading animates, which reading reestablishes—through its animation—in the life of a presence. Something that is, on the lowest level, the presence of a content or of a signified thing; then, on a higher level, the presence of a form, of a signifying thing or of an operation; and, on a higher level still, the development of a system of relations that is always there already, if only as a future possibility. The book rolls up time, unrolls time, and contains this unrolling as the continuity of a presence in which present, past, and future become actual.

4. *The absence of the book* revokes all continuity of presence, just as it evades the questioning conveyed by the book. It is not the interiority of the book, nor its continuously evaded Meaning. Rather it is outside the book, though it is enclosed in it, not so much its exterior as a reference to an outside that does not concern the book.

The more the Work assumes meaning and acquires ambition, retaining in itself not only all works, but all the forms of discourse and all the powers of discourse, the more the absence of the work seems about to propose itself, though without ever allowing itself to be designated. This happens with Mallarmé. With Mallarmé, the Work becomes aware of itself and so knows itself as something coinciding with the absence of the work, the latter then deflecting it from ever coinciding with itself, and dooming it to impossibility. A deviation in which the work disappears into the absence of the work, but in which the absence of the work always escapes the more it reduces itself to being nothing but the Work that has always disappeared already.

5. The act of writing is related to the absence of the work, but is invested in the Work as book. The insanity of writing—*the insane game*—is the relationship of writing, a relationship established not between writing and the production of the book, but, through the production of the book, between the act of writing and the absence of the work.

To write is to produce absence of the work (worklessness). Or: writing is the absence of the work as it *produces itself* through the work and throughout the work. Writing as worklessness (in the active sense of the word) is the insane game, the indeterminacy that lies between reason and unreason.

What happens to the book during this "game," in which worklessness is set loose during the operation of writing? The book: the passage of an infinite movement, a movement that goes from writing as an operation to writing as worklessness; a passage that immediately impedes. Writing passes through the book, but the book is not that to which it is destined (its destiny). Writing passes through the book, completing itself there even as it disappears in the book; and yet, we do not write for the book. The book: a ruse by which writing goes towards *the absence of the book*.

6. Let us try to gain a clearer understanding of the relation of the book to *the absence of the book*.

a) The book plays a dialectical role. In some sense it is there so that not only the dialectic of discourse can take place, but also discourse as dialectic. The book is the work language performs on itself: as though the book were necessary in order for language to become aware of language, for it to know itself and complete itself in its incompleteness.

b) Yet the book that has become a work—the whole literary process, whether it asserts itself as a long succession of books or is manifested in one unique book or in the space that takes the place of that book—is both more of a book than the others and already beyond the book, outside its category and outside its dialectic. *More* a book: a book of knowledge scarcely exists as a book, as a developed volume; the work, on the other hand, makes a claim to be singular: unique, irreplaceable, it is almost a person; this is why there is a dangerous tendency for the work to promote itself into a masterpiece, and also to make itself essential, that is, to designate itself by a signature (it is not only signed by the author, but also somehow by itself, which is more serious). And yet it is already outside the book process: as though the work only indicated the opening—the interruption—through which the neutrality of writing passes, as though the work were oscillating suspended between itself (the totality of language) and an affirmation that had not yet been made.

What is more, in the work, language is already changing direction— or place: place of direction—no longer the logos that participates in a dialectic and knows itself, rather, it is engaged in a different relationship. So that one can say the work hesitates between the book, vehicle of knowledge and fleeting moment of language, and the Book, raised to the Capital Letter, Idea, and Absolute of the book—and then between the work as presence and the absence of the work that is constantly escaping and in which time as time is disturbed.

7. The end of the act of writing does not lie in the book or in the work. As we write the work, we are drawn by the absence of the work. We necessarily fall short of the work, but this does not mean that because of this deficiency we fall under the necessity of the absence of the work.

8. The book: a ruse by which the energy of writing, relying on discourse and allowing itself to be carried along by the vast continuity of discourse, separating itself from it at the limit, is also the use of discourse, restoring to culture that alteration which threatens it and opens it to the absence of the book. Or the book is a labor through which writing, changing the givens of a culture, of "experience," of knowledge, that is to say of discourse, obtains another product that will constitute a new modality of discourse as a whole and will integrate itself with it even as it claims to disintegrate it.

The absence of the book: reader, you would like to be its author, and then you would be nothing more than the plural reader of the Work.

How long will it last—this lack that is sustained by the book and that expels the book from itself as book? Produce the book, then, so that it will detach itself, disengage itself as it scatters: this will not mean that you have produced *the absence of the book*.

9. The book (the civilization of the book) declares: there is a memory that transmits things, there is a system of relations that arranges things; time becomes entangled in the book, where the void still belongs to a structure. But the absence of the book is not based on writing that leaves a mark and determines a directed movement, whether this movement develops linearly from a beginning toward an end, or is deployed from a center toward the surface of a sphere. The absence of the book makes an appeal to writing that does not commit itself, that does not settle out, is not satisfied with disavowing itself, nor with going back over its tracks to erase them.

What summons us to write, when the time of the book determined by the beginning-end relation, and the space of the book determined by deployment from a center, cease to impose themselves? The attraction of (pure) exteriority.

The time of the book, determined by the beginning-end (past-future) relation based on a presence. The space of the book determined by deployment from a center, itself conceived as the search for a source.

Everywhere that there is a system of relations that arranges, a memory that transmits, everywhere that writing gathers in the substance of a mark that reading regards in the light of a meaning (tracing it back to an origin whose sign it is), when emptiness itself belongs to a structure and allows itself to be adjusted, then there is the book: the *law* of the book.

As we write, we always write in the name of the exteriority of writing and against the exteriority of the law, and always the law uses what is written as a resource.

The attraction of (pure) exteriority—the place where, since the outside "precedes" any interior, writing does not deposit itself in the manner of a spiritual or ideal presence subsequently inscribing itself and then leaving a mark, a mark or a sedimentary deposit that would allow one to track it down, in other words to restore it—on the basis of that mark as deficiency—to its ideal presence or ideality, its fullness, its integrity as presence.

Writing marks but leaves no mark; it does not allow us to work our way back from some vestige or sign to anything more than itself as (pure) exteriority and, as such, never given as either forming itself, or being gathered in a unifying relationship with a presence (to be seen, to be heard), or with the whole of presence or the Unique, present-absence.

When we begin to write, either we are not beginning or we are not writing: writing does not accompany beginning.

10. In the book, the uneasiness of writing—the energy—tries to come to rest in the favor of the work (*ergon*), but the absence of the work always summons it immediately to respond to the deflection of the outside, where what is affirmed no longer finds its measure in a relationship of unity.

We have no "idea" of the absence of the work, certainly not as a presence, but also not as the destruction of the thing that would prevent this absence, if only in the form of absence itself. To destroy the work, which itself is not, to destroy at least the affirmation of the work and the dream of the work, to destroy the indestructible, to destroy nothing so that an idea that is out of place here will not impose itself—the idea that to destroy would be enough. The negative can no longer be operative where an affirmation has been made that affirms the work. And in no case can the negative lead to the absence of the work.

Reading would be reading in the book the absence of the book, and as a consequence producing this absence where there is no question of the book being absent or present (defined by an absence or a presence).

The absence of the book: never contemporaneous with the book, not because it emerges from another time, but because it is the source of noncontemporaneity from which it, too, comes. The absence of the book: always diverging, always lacking a present relationship with itself, so that it is never received in its fragmentary plurality by a single reader in the present of his reading, unless, at the limit, with the present torn apart, dissuaded—

The attraction of (pure) exteriority or the vertigo of space as distance, fragmentation that only drives us back to the fragmentary.

The absence of the book: the prior deterioration of the book, the game of dissidence it plays with reference to the space in which it is inscribed; the preliminary dying of the book. Writing, the relation to every book's *other*, to what is de-scription in the book, a scripturary demand beyond discourse, beyond language. The act of writing at the edge of the book, outside the book.

Writing outside language, writing which would be in some sense originally language making it impossible for there to be any object (present or absent) of language. Then writing would never be man's writing, which is to say it would never be God's writing either; at most it would be the writing of the other, of dying itself.

11. The book begins with the Bible, in which the logos is inscribed as law. Here the book achieves its unsurpassable meaning, including what extends beyond it everywhere and cannot be surpassed. The Bible takes language back to its origin: whether this language is written or spoken, it is always the theological era that opens with this language and lasts as long as biblical space and time. The Bible not only offers us the highest model of a book, the specimen that will never be superceded; the Bible also encompasses all books, no matter how alien they are to biblical revelation, knowledge, poetry, prophecy, proverbs, because it contains the spirit of the book; the books that follow it are always contemporaneous with the Bible: the Bible certainly grows, expands with itself in an infinite growth that leaves it identical, permanently sanctioned by the relationship of Unity, just as the ten Laws set forth and contain the monologos, the One Law, the law of Unity that cannot be transgressed and never can be denied by negation alone.

The Bible: a testamentary book in which the alliance is declared, that is to say, the destiny of speech bound to the one who bestows language, and in which he consents to remain through this gift that is the gift of his name, that is to say, also the destiny of this relationship of speech to language, which is dialectic. It is not because the Bible is a sacred book that the books which spring from it—the whole literary process—are marked with the theological sign and cause us to belong to the realm of the theological. It is just the opposite: it was because the testament—the alliance of speech—was rolled up in a book, took the form and structure of a book, that the "sacred" (what is separated from writing) found its place in theology. The book is in essence theological. This is why the first manifestation of the theological (and the only one that continues to unfold and to develop) could only have been in the form of a book. In some sense God does not remain God (does not become divine) except as He speaks through the book.

Mallarmé, confronting the Bible in which God is God, establishes a work in which *the insane game of writing* sets to work and already disowns itself, encountering indeterminacy with its double game: necessity, accident. The Work, the absolute of the voice and of writing, is unworked even before it has been accomplished, before it ruins the possibility of accomplishment by being accomplished. The Work still belongs to the book, and because of this it helps sustain the biblical aspect of every Work, and yet designates the disjunction of a time and a space that are *something other*, precisely that which can no longer assert that it is in a relationship of unity. The Work as book leads Mallarmé outside his name. The Work in which the absence of the work is in effect leads the man who is no longer called Mallarmé to madness: let us understand, if we can, that this *to* means the limit which would be decisive madness if it were crossed; and this obliges us to conclude that the limit—"the edge of madness"—if conceived as indecision that cannot decide, or as non-madness, is more essentially mad: would be abyss, not the abyss, but the edge of the abyss.

Suicide: what is written as necessity in the book is denounced as chance in the absence of the book. What one says, the other repeats, and this statement that reiterates, by virtue of this reiteration encompasses death—the death of self.

12. The anonymity of the book is such that in order to sustain the book it calls for the dignity of a name. The name is that of a temporary particularity that supports reason and that reason authorizes by raising it to itself. The relationship of the Book and the name is always contained in the historical relationship that linked absolute knowledge of system with Hegel's name: this relationship of the Book and of Hegel, identifying the latter with the book, carrying him along in its development, made Hegel into post-Hegel, Hegel-Marx, and then Marx radically estranged from Hegel, who continues to write, to correct, to know, to assert the absolute law of written discourse.

Just as the Book takes the name of Hegel, the work, in its more essential (more uncertain) anonymity, takes the name of Mallarmé, with the difference that Mallarmé not only recognizes the anonymity of the Work as his own trait and the indication of his own place, not only withdraws into this manner of being anonymous, but does not call himself the author of the Work, suggesting at the very most, hyperbolically, that he is the capacity—never a unique or a unifiable capacity—to read the nonpresent Work, that is, the capacity to respond, by his absence, to the work that continues to be absent (but the absent work is not *the absence of the work,* is even separated from it by a radical break).

In this sense, there is already a decisive distance between Hegel's book and Mallarmé's work, a difference evidenced by their different ways of being anonymous in the naming and signing of their works. Hegel does not die, even if he disavows himself in the displacement or reversal of the System: every system still names him, Hegel is never altogether without a name. Mallarmé and the work have no relationship, and this lack of relationship is played out in the Work, establishing the work as what would be forbidden to this particular Mallarmé as to anyone else with a name, and ultimately forbidden to the work when conceived as capable of completing itself by and through itself. The Work is not freed of the name because it could be produced without someone producing it, but because anonymity affirms that it is constantly already beyond whatever could name it. The book is the whole, whatever the form of that totality, whether or not the structure of that totality is completely different from that which a belated reading assigns to Hegel. The Work is not everything, it is already outside everything, but, in its resignation, it is still designated as absolute. The Work is not bound up with success (with completion) as the book is, but with disaster: but this disaster is yet another affirmation of the absolute.

Let us say briefly that the book can always be signed, it remains indifferent to who signs it; the work—Festivity as disaster—requires resignation, requires that whoever claims to write it renounce himself and cease to designate himself.

Then why do we sign our books? Out of modesty, as a way of saying: these are still only books, indifferent to signatures.

13. The "absence of the book"—which the written thing provokes as the future of writing, a future that has never come to pass—does not form a concept anymore than the word "outside" does, or the word "fragment," or the word "neuter," but it helps conceptualize the word "book." It is not some contemporary expositor who gives Hegel's philosophy its coherence and conceives of it as a book, thus conceiving of the book as the finality of absolute Knowledge; beginning at the end of the 19th century, it is Mallarmé. But Mallarmé, through the very force of his experience, immediately pierces through the book to designate (dangerously) the Work whose center of attraction—a center that is always off center—would be writing. The act of writing, *the insane game.* But the act of writing has a relationship, a relationship of otherness, with the absence of the Work, and it is precisely because he senses this radical alteration that comes to writing and through writing with the absence of the Work that Mallarmé is able to name the Book, naming it as the thing that gives meaning to becoming by suggesting a place and a time for it: first and last concept. But Mallarmé does not yet name the absence of the book or he only recognizes it as a way of thinking the Work, the Work as failure or impossibility.

14. *The absence of the book* is not the book coming apart, even though in some sense coming apart lies at the origin of the book and is its opposing principle. The fact that the book is always coming apart (disordering itself) still only leads to another book or to a possibility other than the book, but not to the absence of the book. Let us admit that what

obsesses the book (what haunts it) would be the absence of the book that it always lacks, contenting itself with containing it (holding it at a distance) without containing it (transforming it into content). Let us also admit the opposite, that the book encloses the absence of the book that excludes it, but that the absence of the book is never conceived only on the basis of the book and only as its negation. Let us admit that if the book carries meaning, the absence of the book is so alien to meaning that nonmeaning does not concern it either.

It is very striking that within a certain tradition of the book (the one derived from the kabbalists' formulation, although there it is a question of sanctioning the mystical signification of the literal presence), what is called the "written Torah" preceded the "oral Torah," the latter then giving rise to the edited version that alone constitutes the Book. Here, thought is confronted with an enigmatic proposition: Nothing precedes writing. Yet the writing on the first tablets does not become readable until after they are broken and because they are broken—after and because of the resumption of the oral decision, which brings us to the second writing, the one we know, rich in meaning, capable of issuing commandments, always equal to the law it transmits.

Let us try to examine this surprising proposition by relating it to what might be a future experiment of writing. There are two kinds of writing, one white, the other black; one makes the invisibility of a colorless flame invisible, the other is made accessible in the form of letters, characters, and articulations by the power of the black fire. Between the two there is orality, which, however, is not independent, but always involved with the second kind of writing, because it is the black fire itself, the measured darkness that limits, defines all light, makes all light visible. Thus, what we call oral is designation in a temporal present and a presence of space, but also, at first, development or mediation as it is guaranteed by a discourse that explains, welcomes and defines the neutrality of the initial inarticulation. The "oral Torah" is therefore no less written, but is called oral in the sense that as discourse it alone allows there to be communication, otherwise known as *commentary*, speech that both teaches and declares, authorizes and justifies: as though language (discourse) were necessary for writing to give rise to common legibility and perhaps also to the Law understood as prohibition and limit; and also as though the first writing, in its configuration of invisibility, had to be considered *outside speech* and directed only towards the *outside,* an absence or a fracture so primordial that it will have to be broken to escape the savagery of what Hölderlin calls the aorgic.

15. Writing is absent from the Book, being the nonabsent absence on the basis of which the Book, having absented itself from this absence, makes itself readable (on both its levels—the oral and the written, the Law and its exegesis, the forbidden and the thought of the forbidden) and comments on itself by enclosing history: the closing of the book, the severity of the letter, the authority of knowledge. What we can say about this writing, which is absent from the book and yet stands in a relationship of otherness with it, is that it remains alien to readability, that it is unreadable insofar as to read is necessarily to enter through one's gaze into a relationship of meaning or nonmeaning with a presence. There would, therefore, be a writing exterior to the kind of knowledge that is gained through reading, and also exterior to the form and the requirements of the Law. Writing, (pure) exteriority, alien to every relationship of presence, and to all legality.

The moment the exteriority of writing *slackens,* that is, responds to the appeal of the oral force, agreeing to be informed in language giving rise to the book—the written discourse—this exteriority tends to appear as the exteriority of the Law, on the highest level, and on the lowest level as the interiority of meaning. The Law is writing itself which has renounced the exteriority of interlocution to designate the place of the interdicted. The illegitimacy of writing, always rebellious towards the Law, hides the asymmetrical illegitimacy of the Law in relation to writing.

Writing: exteriority. Perhaps there is a "pure" exteriority of writing, but this is only a postulate, a postulate that is already disloyal to the neutrality of writing. In the book that signs our alliance with every Book, exteriority does not succeed in authorizing itself on its own, and as it writes down its name, it does so under the space of the Law. The exteriority of writing, spreading itself out in layers in the book, becomes exteriority as law. The Book speaks as Law. Reading it, we read in it that everything which is, is either forbidden or allowed. But isn't this structure of permission and prohibition a result of our level of reading? Isn't there perhaps another reading of the Book in which the book's other would cease to be proclaimed in precepts? And if we were to read this way, would we read yet another book? Wouldn't we be about to read *the absence of the book?*

The initial exteriority: perhaps we should assume that its nature is such that we would not be able to tolerate it except under the sanction of the Law. What would happen if the system of prohibition and limitations stopped protecting it? Or might it simply be there, at the limit of possibility, just to make the limit possible? Is this exteriority nothing more than a requirement of limit? Is limit itself conceived only through a definition that is necessary at the approach of the unlimited and that would disappear if it was ever passed—for that reason impassable, yet always passed because it is impassable?

16. Writing contains exteriority. The exteriority that becomes Law falls henceforth under the protection of the Law—which, in turn, is written; that is, once again under the protection of writing. We must assume that this reduplication of writing, which immediately designates it as difference, only affirms, through this duplicity, the quality of exteriority itself, which is always developing, always exterior to itself, in a relationship of discontinuity. There is a "first" writing, but since this writing is the first writing, it is already distinct from itself, separated because of what marks it, being at the same time nothing but that mark and also different from it, if the mark is made there, and broken, out-distanced, and denounced to such a degree—in that outside, that dis-junction where it is revealed—that a new rupture will be necessary, a break that is violent but human (and, in this sense, defined and delimited), so that, having become an explosive text—and the initial fragmentation having been replaced by a determined act of rupture—the law may, under the mask of the forbidden, redeem a promise of unity.

In other words, the breaking of the first tablets is not a break with an original state of undivided harmony; on the contrary, what it initiates is the substitution of a limited exteriority (in which the possibility of a limit is intimated) for an exteriority without limitation, the substitution of a lack for an absence, of a break for a gap, of an infraction for the pure-impure fraction of the fragmentary, the fraction that falls short of the sacred separation, crowding into the scission of the neuter (which is the neuter). To put it yet another way, we must break with the first exteriority so that language, henceforth regularly divided, in a reciprocal bond of mastery with itself, grammatically constructed, will engage us in mediate and immediate relationships with the second exteriority, in which the logos is law and the law logos—relationships that guarantee discourse and then dialectic, where the law in turn will dissolve.

The "first" writing, far from being more immediate than the second, is alien to all these categories. It does not bestow its gifts generously through some ecstatic participation in which the law that protects the One merges with it and ensures confusion with it. The first writing is otherness itself, a severity and austerity that never grant authority, the burning of a parching breeze, infinitely more rigorous than any law. The law is what saves us from writing by forcing writing to act indirectly through the rupture—the transitiveness—of speech. A salvation that introduces us to knowledge and, through our desire for knowledge, even to the Book, where knowledge maintains desire by hiding it from itself.

17. The nature of the Law: it is infringed upon even before it has been stated; from that time on, certainly, it is promulgated in a high place, at a distance and in the name of what is distant, but without any relationship of direct knowledge with those for whom it is destined. From this we could conclude that the law, as it is transmitted, tolerates transmission, becomes a law of transmission, is only constituted as a law by the decision to fail to do so: there would be no limit if the limit were not passed, revealed as impassable by being passed.

Yet doesn't the law precede all knowledge (including knowledge of the law), knowledge which it alone opens, preparing it for its conditions by a preliminary "it must be," even if only from the Book in which the law attests to itself through the order—the structure—that it looms over as it establishes it?

Always anterior to the law, neither founded in nor determined by the necessity of being brought to knowledge, never endangered by someone's misunderstanding, always essentially affirmed by the infraction that implies reference to it, attracting in its trial the authority that submits itself to it, and all the more firm because it is open to easy transgression: the law.

The law's "it must be" is not primarily a "thou shalt." "It must be" applies to no one or, more deliberately, applies only to no one. The nonapplicability of the law is not only a sign of its abstract force, of its inexhaustible authority, of the reserve it maintains. Incapable of saying *thou*, the law is never directed at anyone in particular: not because it is universal, but because it separates in the name of unity, being separation itself that prescribes for the sake of what is unique. This is perhaps the law's august lie: itself having "legalized" the outside in order to make it possible (or real), it frees itself of all determination and all content in order to preserve itself as pure inapplicable form, pure exigency to which no presence is able to respond, yet immediately particularized in multiple norms and, through the code of alliance, in ritual forms so as to allow for the discreet interiority of a return to self, where the infrangible intimacy of the "thou shalt" will be affirmed.

18. The ten laws are only laws with reference to Unity. God—the name that cannot be spoken in vain because no language can contain it—is only God so that He can carry the Unity and designate its sovereign finality. No one will try to attack the One. And then the Other bears witness, bears witness for none other than the Unique, a reference that unites all thought to what is *un*thought, keeping it turned towards the One as towards something upon which thought cannot infringe. It is therefore important to say: not the unique God, but Unity is necessarily God, transendence itself.

The exteriority of the law finds its measure in responsibility towards the One, it is an alliance of the One and the many that thrusts aside as impious the primordiality of difference. Yet in the law itself there is still a clause that retains some memory of the exteriority of writing, when it is said: thou shalt make no images, thou shalt not represent, thou shalt reject presence in the form of resemblance, sign, and mark. What does that mean? First, and almost too clearly, the prohibition of the sign as mode of presence. The act of writing—if that act is relating oneself to the image and naming the idol—makes its mark outside the exteriority proper to it, an exteriority that writing then repels in its effort to overwhelm it, both by the void of words and by the pure signification of the sign. "Thou shalt make no idol" is thus, in the form of the law, not a statement about the law, but about the exigency of writing that precedes any law.

19. Let us admit that the law is obsessed by exteriority, that this obsession haunts it and that it separates itself from this obsession, in the name of the very separation that establishes it as a form, in the movement in which this obsession formulates it as law. Let us admit that exteriority as writing, a relation always without relation, can be called exteriority that *slackens* into law, precisely when it is *more tense*, when it has the tension of a gathering form. We need to know that as soon as the law exists (finds its place), everything changes, and it is the so-called "initial" exteriority that—in the name of a law that from now on cannot be denounced—is presented as slackness, as undemanding neutrality, in the same way that writing outside the law, outside the book, seems at that point to be nothing more than the return to a spontaneity without rules, an automatism of ignorance, an irresponsible gesture, an immoral game. To put it another way, one cannot climb back up from exteriority as law to exteriority as writing; going back up, in this context, would be going down. That is to say: one cannot "go back up" save by accepting the fall—though one is incapable of consenting to it—an essentially indeterminate fall into inessential chance (what the law disdainfully calls a game—a game in which everything is risked each time, and everything is lost: the necessity of law, the chance of writing). The law is the summit, there is no other. Writing remains outside the arbitration between high and low.[1]

---

[1] I dedicate (*and disavow*) these uncertain pages to the books in which the absence of the book is already being produced by being promised; these books were written by———, but will only be designated here by the lack of a name, for the sake of friendship.

Afterword

Afterword
by P. Adams Sitney

1. The Invisible Author

Ut pictura poesis: this slogan out of Horace has reassured us with a comforting definition of literature for centuries. One measure of the exacting phrase, the precise word, has always been the vividness and strength of its image. In secular culture the term "Imagination" has an almost sacred weight; statements of the highest aspirations of art, literary or not, attest its continued worth. Visibility seems to be one literary value that is self-evident. Even the Symbolist exaltation of the hint over bold representation confirms the primacy of vision; it is too important and holy to be proferred promiscuously; the poem should withhold it and unfold it as a ritual of mystery. Yet the centrality of a poetics of vision has in our time come into question. The very obviousness and the comforting assurance that the optical reflex to reading is a value, has been subjected to doubt. Perhaps a "darker" truth lurks behind this self-evidential value. Even the investigation is hampered and often made paradoxical by the traditional vocabulary of truth which is a network of metaphors for light and sight. In Maurice Blanchot's meditations on the nature of literary language, that which resists or refuses to become visible is teased and drawn toward the reader's attention, in a style made torturously difficult by the lack of a vocabulary or a tradition for articulating the nature of this blind invisibility.

Maurice Blanchot is a man about whom almost nothing is known. To my knowledge he has never lectured, read in public, granted an interview, or written an autobiographical paragraph. In Pierre de Boisdeffre's *Dictionnaire de littérature contemporaine* 1900-1960, his is one of the rare entries without a photograph (the reclusive Henri Michaux was another).* The biographical information begins and ends with his birth: September 22, 1907, Quain (Saône et Loire). No other reference book has more than that about him.

In his twenties Blanchot was a journalist and activist of the French right. In 1968 he marched in support of the student insurrection, the most glorious moment of the modern French Left. Attempts have been made to dredge up political articles he wrote in the thirties as if they were keys to the enigma of his literary persona, but they have turned out to be transparently impotent attempts to cope with a vacuum.

Death, the obsessive mystery at the center of Blanchot's work, will inevitably reveal the outline of his life. Longevity has insured the suppression of even a rudimentary biography. Yet I suspect there is not much more to know than what we can reasonably guess. There is evidence of a sound academic training, probably in German philology. Rumors of a serious and protracted illness have emerged to account for his "invisibility." His long friendship with Georges Bataille, with whom he collaborated on the journal Critique, appears to have been a matter of mutual admiration and a shared fascination with German philosophy and radicalism in literature.

For thirty years, from the forties into the seventies, Blanchot's literary meditations appeared quite regularly in the most prominent French publications. Perhaps only Edmund Wilson commanded the authority and showed the consistency of insight for American readers that Blanchot held for the French. There is not a significant aspect of modern French literature that Blanchot did not examine in his regular contributions, first to Le Journal des Débats, and later to the Nouvelle Revue Française. Sartre, Ponge, Char, Camus, Bataille, Klossowski, Beckett,

---

*The presence of an image on the cover of the Station Hill Press edition of Death Sentence, Lydia Davis's translation of L'Arrêt de mort, Blanchot's first book-length récit, did not escape the author's attention. In a note to the translator he acknowledged receipt of a copy with gracious praise for her work and, referring to the high contrast photograph of a virtually unrecognizable woman, printed in silver and black ink, he added with gnomic ambiguity, "Quant à la présentation, j'aurais préféré que le visage restât l'invisible où il s'est éffacé. Mais l'invisible demeure cependant." ("As for the design, I would have preferred that nothing could be seen of the face where it faded away. But the invisible remains nevertheless.")

Robbe-Grillet, Lévi-Strauss, Foucault, Leiris, Lacan received sympathetic and judicious scrutiny from him. His examinations of the unfolding of contemporary French literature and thought were interspersed with meditations on the authors who have consistently preoccupied him: Mallarmé, Lautréamont, Sade, Hegel, Hölderlin, Nietzsche, and Kafka. The secondary literature on these writers has often provided the pretext for a reexamination of their relevance for Blanchot. Yet another dimension of his critical position has been the presentation of German authors to the French public: Mann, Broch, Musil, Brecht, Döblin, Rilke, Hesse and Benjamin. Less frequently he directed his attention to English and American authors: there are major essays on Blake, James, Woolf, Faulkner, Henry Miller.

In presenting these authors Blanchot seldom offered an interpretation. He is not a philologist, and a collection of his essays on the Germans or the English would be less than useless; in fact, it would betray his enterprise. In those weekly, later monthly, literary meditations of three decades Blanchot would situate an author. Yet this placing had as little to do with literary history as with philology. Volume after volume, fiction, poetry, or philosophy, that Blanchot read constituted an eruption of that instability in language we call literature. Blanchot drew the reader's attention to the tensions and paradoxes from which literature originates. That is why he was so rarely a critic. The few times that the derogatory tone enters his essays — the discussion of Sartre's novels is one example — it comes forcefully to divert attention from the thematic surface of the novel or poem to the essential literary problem obscured by the work. The books and authors Blanchot championed most enthusiastically were always those that demonstrated "this insane game of writing."

Even while Blanchot was presenting, or perhaps more precisely confirming, the major figures of modern literature for a broad intellectual public in France, he was subordinating them to the mystery of "literature" which preoccupied him. It was not an issue of the formation of a modern canon. The books he discussed were selected with consistent taste and high standards, but they constituted a conservative list. Only in his first collection of essays, *Faux Pas* (1948), do we find him taking risks as a critic in the rather banal sport of supporting new and unestablished writers. That initial phase of his critical work, when he wistfully anticipated the emergence of a Mallarméan novel, coincided with his own first efforts as a writer of fiction. *Thomas l'obscur, Aminadab*, and *Le Trés Haut*, his longest works of fiction and the only books he called *"romans"* (novels), still revolve around the kinds of characters and situations, and more importantly the psychological perspectives, familiar in the novels of Giraudoux, to whom he was indebted, and Kafka, whose work he claimed not to know at that time.

The publication of *Faux Pas* marks Blanchot's transition from enlightened literary journalism to theory. He assembled short essays he had contributed to the *Journal des Débats* over the previous decade into groups which gave his reviews of primarily recent novels the semblance of continuous reflection on the genre and lent a similar cohesiveness to his writings on poetry. Far more important than this editorial montage was his decision to introduce the volume with a long theoretical article on the nature of authorship. "From Dread to Language" was Blanchot's first sustained investigation of the mystery of literary language. It is both the product of his energetic and brilliant reviews and the starting point of his mature work.

Faux Pas had been preceded by two books, the "novels" *Thomas l'obscur* and *Aminadab*. He was yet to write *Le Trés Haut*, his last and most traditional *roman*. Its publication in 1948 and that of his second collection of essays, *La Part du feu* in 1949 would complete the first stage of his maturity and establish Blanchot as one of the most formidable literary figures in France after the war.

Blanchot never won the recognition that Sartre and Merleau-Ponty and later the writers of the *nouveau roman* got outside of France. In the late forties, the *Yale French Studies* translated two of his shorter articles from *La Part du feu*, and described him as "the most important critic in France." But the American public that devoured Sartre and later were to buy impressive numbers of translated essays by Barthes and Derrida, never had a chance to read Blanchot. His aloofness from the academic world may have contributed to this neglect, which his closest ally, Bataille, shared. Timing seems to have had more to do with it. Blanchot came into the fullness of his powers at the end of the 1940s, but the fifties, the period of his greatest influence and most striking originality, was a time when American readers and publishers showed little interest in theoretical discourse. The major works of phenomenology were still untranslated then.

The nearest Blanchot came to conventional scholarship was his long study *Lautréamont et Sade* (1949) which included an edition of *Les Chants de Maldoror*. But at that time neither author was available to English readers. *Horizon* published a translation of the Sade material the same year, and more than a decade later Grove Press used a long Blanchot essay as the preface to their translation of *120 Days of Sodom*. In both cases the fascination of Sade had more to do with the publication in English than Blanchot's insights. In fact, the long essay in the Grove Press edition seems to have been included to insure against lawsuits for publishing Sade; Blanchot was an implicit witness to "redeeming social value."

Lautréamont had been a presence in Blanchot's criticism from the beginning. In *Faux Pas* he set up *Les Chants de Maldoror* and the prose of Mallarmé as twin models for the kind of novels he hoped would appear after the war. In 1948 Blanchot responded to his own appeal for a radical renovation of the "tradition" of Lautréamont—Breton's *Nadja* would have to be part of that elusive continuity—with the publication of the *récit*, *L'Arrêt de mort*. The same year he published *Le Très Haut*. The latter looks back to the first novels Blanchot published during the occupation, while the former indicated the direction his fiction would take subsequently. In a remarkable gesture of self-revision he published a new version of *Thomas l'obscur* in 1950. The transformation of the novel into a *récit* was almost entirely an act of elimination: he pared down sentences, eliminated characters, suppressed psychological perspectives; he excavated from the discursiveness of a very uncanny novel an even more startling work.

The development of Blanchot's criticism corresponded to the changes in his fiction. *Faux Pas*, as I have noted, was composed of essays he wrote in the late thirties and early forties for the *Journal des Débats* and *L'Insurge*. The essays he wrote for *L'Arche* (Gide's magazine), *Les Temps Modernes* (Sartre's), and *Critique* (Bataille's) in the next few years were gathered into *La Part du feu* (1949). These essays are longer than those of the earlier collection. The post-war journals provided Blanchot as much space as he needed to develop his ideas. *Critique*, which Bataille founded and edited, was ostensibly a journal of book reviews. In it, current works of theoretical interest — publications in philosophy, sociology, psychoanalysis, art history, etc., and French translations of major works of foreign literature — were given exhaustive critical attention. The most important essay of *La Part du feu*, the theoretical conclusion of the volume, which like the introduction to *Faux Pas* he printed in italics, had appeared in two numbers of *Critique* in 1948 and 1949. They were Blanchot's response to the revival of interest in Hegel occasioned by the publication of the major studies by Hippolyte and Kojève. They were not in any sense reviews of those books. Bataille recognized this and published a more direct evaluation of those seminal books in the very issue in which the first of Blanchot's two articles appeared.

Critique was a useful format for Blanchot, since he grounded his literary theory in responding to contemporary developments in literary and intellectual life. However the real situation for him, and the vehicle through which he produced his most significant theoretical work, arose with the revival of the *Nouvelle Revue Française* in 1953. In a series called "recherches" Blanchot contributed an essay to that monthly with decreasing regularity for fifteen years. In the one hundred and eighty numbers that appeared through 1967 Blanchot contributed to one hundred and fifteen. Blanchot immediately began to utilize the freedom the N.R.F. offered him. A remarkable series of articles on the nature of writing and reading, "work" and book, appeared in the first two years of the journal's renewed existence. Blanchot interspersed these texts with longer exegetical essays on Rilke, Mallarmé, and Kafka (mostly from *Critique*, where he continued to publish through 1953) in his first critical volume of the highest order, *L'Espace littéraire* (1955). A second collection of *N.R.F.* essays, *Le Livre à venir*, followed in 1959, this time stressing texts on novelists and offering a theory of the *récit*. It was during this same period that Blanchot wrote his own *récits: Au Moment voulu* (1951), *Celui qui ne m'accompagnait pas* (1952) and *Le Dernier Homme* (1957).

After that both his fiction and his criticism took another turn. The first sign of this shift was the contribution he made to a Festschrift for

Heidegger's seventieth birthday, "L'Attente."This series of aphorisms about expectation and temporality turned up three years later as a part of his last *récit*: *L'Attente l'oubli* (1962), an abstract fiction purged of personality, devoid of narrative, in which two voices discuss and occupy time. There is as little authentic dialogue between these two voices as there is in the Baltimore Catechism, but considerably more skepticism.

Blanchot, the man who never gives an interview, greeted his surprised readers in the *N.R.F.* during the first months of 1960 with an interview of himself. His essay on the change of the decade began thus:

> Will you admit this fact: that we are at a turning point?
> —If it's a fact, it's not a turning point.

Thus his dialogue with himself continues, even to the comic moment in which one voice accuses the other of "speaking like a book." The contradictions and reformulations which had characterized all of Blanchot's earlier essays here turn into a critical dialogue through a change that is hardly more than orthographic. Unlike the Platonic tradition, with its venerable repetitions within the history of philosophy, these two voices insist only on maintaining the same position.

Throughout the sixties such dialogues became a part of Blanchot's critical contributions to the *N.R.F.* The speakers were always the same: Blanchot and himself. In 1969 he organized these dialogues along with his recent discursive essays into his longest and most impressive theoretical book, *L'Entretien infini*. The subsequent volume of essays, *L'Amitié*, was much weaker.

At seventy Blanchot issued *Le Pas au-delà*, a closer blending of fiction and philosophy than *L'Entretien infini*. In this very recent book the preoccupation with Nietzsche's concept of the Eternal Return, which can be traced through many of the essays Blanchot published in the sixties, reaches a climax. Its tone is valedictory. It seemed as though this mysterious author intended it to be his last book. Yet while this present collection of his essays in English was being typeset he released *L'Ecriture du désastre*.

2. The Terror of the Text

At the end of the "Note" which prefaces *L'Entretien infini*, Blanchot warns us: "Then writing becomes a terrible responsibility. Invisibly, writing is called upon to unmake the discourse in which we remain, we who dispose of it—we are so hapless that we believe we are comfortably installed in it. To write, from this perspective, is the greatest violence, for it breaks the Law, every law and its own law." By suppressing his biography and effacing his authorial personality Maurice Blanchot has foregrounded the terrible responsibility of reading for those drawn to his texts. His radical refusal to assert his authorial prerogatives sometimes puts the reader to the test. He has, for instance, declined to advise or comment upon the editorial selection of essays for this initial presentation of his theoretical work in English. His is a most gracious terrorism. This generous indifference to the fate of his writing is frighteningly consistent with its themes.

In the same introductory "Note" to *L'Entretien infini* Blanchot confesses that his nagging of the question "What is at stake in the fact that something such as art or literature exists?" has covered up "and continues to cover up a secular tradition of estheticism." The status of the "secular tradition" has been a consistent object of Blanchot's researches. Although he writes as an atheist, he often uses the Bible, introducing Latin phrases from the Vulgate as if they were privileged fragments of a metacritical language. The testamental model is particularly important for an understanding of Blanchot's negative mythopoeia because it claims the transcendental authority which he asserts literature always lacks. His Christ is mediator of the problematical relationship between author and reader. In *L'Espace littéraire* the text warns the reader, with a phrase parodying Christ's injunction to Mary Magdelene in the Gospel of John, *Noli me legere*, "Don't read me." In the same book the reader is

called upon to repeat Christ's formula for raising his dead friend from
the grave, from the same Gospel: *"Lazare, veni foras"* (Lazarus, come
forth). These Johanine tomb scenes reappear, beside varying interpretations of the myth of Orpheus, throughout Blanchot's criticism. They are
there to remind us that nothing is more serious than the desperate and
engimatic meetings of readers and texts. For Blanchot insists that the
most sublime stories, our central myths, are allegories of the textual
confrontations which we obsessively avoid.

Of course, Blanchot would not describe those allegories in such crude
and blunt terms. And for the best of reasons. Such critical reductivism
silently reasserts the supervisory authority of the written word, and the
transparency of reading even while it claims the opposite. Blanchot's
sinuous style invites the reader to participate in an event which makes
rituals of those allegories. Furthermore he neglects the validity of allegory as a mode, preferring to reaffirm the Romantic theory of the "symbol."

His first volume of criticism, *Faux Pas*, brings together fifty-four short
articles he wrote for *L'Insurge* (in 1937) and *Le Journal des Débats*
(between 1941 and 1943) in four sections. The first group, "From Dread
to Language," has a lengthy preface, printed in italics, which sets the
program for the volume and for Blanchot's entire critical enterprise in its
initial stage. This essay finds its complement in "Literature and the
Right to Death," which he printed also in italics at the end of his next
collection.

In these two essays Blanchot's critical theories and strategies crystal-
ized; the characteristic movements of his thought reveal themselves
there in an involuted struggle with the very works he would analyze.
Generally he presents and interprets an author by picking up the direction of his thought, extending and skewing his vocabulary, his forms, his
myths, until a moment comes when he suddenly turns away and into
the mannerisms of a different author. Blanchot's dialectical thought
foregrounds itself before the equipoise of the predecessors he invokes. In
an elaborate play of literary allusions he creates a field of tensions in
which his own positions and obsessions can be clarified. The mandarin
obliqueness of these unidentified allusions requires an elaborate
exegesis from American readers. I shall devote more pages of this after-

word to the first two essays of the anthology than to any others, not only because of their obscurities but also because they initiate the themes and strategies which characterize Blanchot's later theory.

In "From Dread to Language" Kierkegaard, Mallarmé, and Balzac successively provide pseudo-structures for his meditation on the relationship of writing to reading. Only the Balzacian model is not specifically identified. However the allusion to his *conte philosophique*, "Le Chef-d'oeuvre inconnu," which terminates the essay, is quite explicit. Thus Blanchot concludes:

> It retains a little meaning from the fact that it never receives all its meaning, and it is filled with dread because it cannot be pure dread. The unknown masterpiece always allows one to see in the corner the tip of a charming foot, and this delicious foot prevents the work from being finished, but also prevents the painter from facing the emptiness of his canvas and saying, with the greatest feeling of repose: "Nothing, nothing! At last, there is nothing."

Blanchot's deliberate misquotation of Balzac's fictional painter, Frenhofer, reverses the meaning of his despairing cry, "Nothing, nothing! And to have worked ten years!" After working for ten years on a realistic painting of an historical woman of incomparable beauty, Balzac's Frenhofer agrees to show his work to Porbus and Poussin (whose names the author drew from art history) on condition that the latter bring his mistress, the exquisite Gilette, to pose nude for him. He wants to compare his painted woman with the most beautiful woman alive. However, when Poussin saw the canvas, a palimpsest of paint obscuring all but one spectacularly rendered foot, he blurted out that he saw nothing on the canvas. Frenhofer despaired; then, deciding that the others were merely jealous, fell back into admiration of the image he made.

Balzac concentrated on the moral dilemma of Gilette and the betrayal she felt upon realizing that Poussin cared more for art than for her. History has conspired with Blanchot to make the story prophetic of the disappearance of the figure in modern painting and of the ambivalent status of representation in modern aesthetics. As Blanchot interprets it, the foot ceases to be a vestige of the painting from its perfect stage, now hopelessly over-labored; instead, it becomes the inescapable referential moment in a purified language (signaled by the quotation of Mallarmé's phrase "to render more pure the words of the tribe"). In this one, final sentence of the essay, a sleight of hand turns Balzac's tale into an allegory of the struggle between novelty and archaic form.

The passion which kept Frenhofer working for ten years on the single painting, his faith in the transcendent perfection of his image as well as the compulsion to test that faith, his despair, and his paranoid-like defense against the suggestion of failure are phases of the dialectic of "dread" even though Blanchot does not spell them out for us. The "dread" out of which the work of art emerges is an aestheticization of the dialectic of Kierkegaard's *The Concept of Dread*. Although it is not the central argument of Kierkegaard's short book, the movement from dread to language is inscribed in its sixth section where the author deals with "Dread as the presupposition of original sin and as explaining it retrogressively by going back to its origin." Kierkegaard's aim is to describe the psychology of sin through a meditation on the Fall as described in Genesis. Blanchot discarded Kierkegaard's context; Adam plays no part in his allegory of the artist; Kierkegaard himself, as a pseudonymous author, surreptitiously enters the essay as yet another model for the writer in "dread." Instead Blanchot portrays "the writer" in a constellation of concepts derived from *The Concept of Dread*: the difficult juncture of dread and language, the dialectic of ambiguity, and the revival of the notion of the demoniacal.

Kierkegaard defines dread with chiastic oxymorons: "Dread is a sympathetic antipathy and an antipathetic sympathy." In Kierkegaard's theory of language, meaning follows expression. Language speaks in Adam but understanding comes retrospectively. Dread is the prelude and ground of subsequent understanding. It coincides with the gift of language and points to the future moment when what has been uttered can be understood.

Whereas Adam's dread, as all dread, was dread of nothing, that is, without an object, the Blanchotian author probes this nothingness. In examining the equivocal status of this nothingness, the model of Balzac's Frenhofer eventually comes to service.

Blanchot treats Frenhofer's canvas as a model for literary language where the tension between transparent mimesis and purely sonorous language can never be resolved. Balzac's painter sought to improve on contemporary actuality with his realistic portrait, projecting his transcendently beautiful woman into the past and into paint. Such idealism, however, only constitutes a negative phase in the history of this work, as Blanchot sees it. The substitution of "at last" for "And to have worked ten years!" underlines the temporal dimension of his interpretation. Balzac ends his story by telling us that Frenhofer burned all of his paintings and died the night of his encounter with the younger painters. Whether he died convinced of his success or his failure is left open to question. In either case his opus of ten years' making was completed. But Blanchot would deny the possibility of completion. As he reads the story, the ten years' labor is a quest for the abolition of the referential human figure, a quest for the nothingness which would annul the "*hasard*" (chance) of the material world.

The wrestling match with "*hasard*" (chance) is yet another part of his inheritance from Mallarmé's poetry and theory. This too he reinterprets from the vantage point of literary events after Mallarmé's death. For Mallarmé "*hasard*" was a name for the rhetorical indeterminacy of representational language. Yet when Blanchot writes of "hasard" the literary practices of the Surrealists are never far from his thoughts. He identifies their search for formal innovation through automatic writing with "le hasard demeure aux termes." In fact, "From Dread to Language" is largely a polemic against the use of chance operations as a short cut to innovation. Although Blanchot's essay meticulously avoids historical arguments and allusions to historical process, literary history creeps into it through the allegorization of the Balzac, Kierkegaard, and Mallarmé texts. He implies that these writers of the 19th century told more than they could know about the problems confronting a writer in 1943.

The allegories of Mallarmé and Balzac which Blanchot superimposes over his reading of Kierkegaard reverse the meaning of nothingness that is found in *The Concept of Dread*. There the dread of nothing is dread of the future, of the lapse into history which is all before Adam, just as the meaning of language is projected as futural. The nothingness that Blanchot found in Mallarmé and imparted to Balzac, on the other hand, comes in the wake of an abolished presence. In the final paragraph of the essay he brings together the temporal and the rhetorical arguments:

> Everything in my mind, therefore, strives to be a necessary connection and a tested value; everything in my memory strives to be the recollection of a language that has not yet been invented and the invention of a language that one recollects; to each operation there corresponds a meaning, and to these operations as a group, that other meaning that there is no distinct meaning for each of them; words have their meaning as the substitute for an idea, but also as a composition of sounds and as a physical reality; images signify themselves as images, and thoughts affirm the twofold necessity that associates them with certain expressions and makes them thoughts of other thoughts.

Five years after the publication of *Faux Pas* Blanchot printed another italicized essay as the conclusion of his similarly titled collection, called *La Part du feu* [The Fire's Share] (as if the operation of criticism were a sacrifice to, or for, a different literary activity). In "Literature and the Right to Death" the confluence of historical and ontological arguments becomes more thematic, for the essay is an ironic aestheticization of Hegel's *The Phenomenology of Mind*. The first part of the essay, under the title "The animal kingdom of the mind," appeared in the same issue of *Critique* as Henri Niet's double review of two then recent and tremendously significant contributions to the study of Hegel, Jean Hyppolite's *Genèse et structure de la Phénoménologie de l'esprit de Hegel* (1946) and Alexandre Kojève's *Introduction à la lecture de Hegel* (1947). Blanchot mentions both books in the footnotes to his essay; they were obviously the immediate source of his near parody of Hegel. Of equal significance to Blanchot's essay was the publication of Emmanuel Lévinas' *De l'Existence à l'existant* (1947) which dominates the second part of the text (called "Literature and the Right to Death") where it too is acknowledged obliquely in footnotes. As Blanchot reads Kojève, Hyppolite, and Lévinas, he is thinking of the same cluster of writers who generally occupy his critical thought: Mallarmé, Lautréamont, Sade, Kafka, and peripherally Ponge.

Since the issue of the essay is the status of literary language, Hegel provides little more than a scaffolding. When Blanchot writes, "As we know a writer's main temptations are called stoicism, scepticism, and the unhappy consciousness," he veers toward self-parody. His tendency to allegorize philosophical texts as parables of writing has attained a degree of flippancy which it fortunately overcomes. Blanchot is, of course, almost totally disinterested in the status of the Hegelian *Begriff* (Miller: "Concept"). But the theory of language which surfaces in the German philosopher's metaphors and is elaborately excavated in Kojève's interpretation immediately echoes for him one of the most famous passages in Mallarmé's prose. At the end of "Crise de vers" the poet imported several paragraphs from his introduction to René Ghil's *Traité du verbe*. There the act of murder which naming performs on things is described with the well known phrase "transposer un fait de nature en sa presque disparition vibratoire selon le jeu de la parole."

> What purpose is served by the miracle of transposing a natural fact into its almost vibratory disappearance by means of the word's action; however, if it is not that there may proceed from it, without the embarrassment of an immediate or concrete reminder, the pure notion.
>
> I say: a flower! and, out of the forgetfulness where my voice banishes any contour, inasmuch as it is something other than known calyxes, musically arises, an idea itself and fragrant, the one absent from all bouquets.[1]

The difference between Hegel and Mallarmé does not concern Blanchot at this point. He associates the two, and Kojève as well, and in so doing he would illuminate the poetics of Hegel through Mallarmé rather than the epistemology of Mallarmé through Hegel.

The substitution of a woman for a flower strikes us more than the parallel substitution of a cat where Kojève writes "dog." The woman who musically rises in this essay suggests the displacement from a *crise de vers* to a *crise du roman* which is a continual concern for Blanchot.

This appears most nakedly in connection with Mallarmé in *Faux Pas* where "Mallarmé et l'art du roman" shows up as the first of eighteen "Digressions sur le roman," a section of the book which constitutes the

[1] Stephane Mallarmé, *Mallarmé*, ed. and trans. Anthony Hartley (London: Penguin, 1965) pp. 174-75.

crux of Blanchot's thoughts on novelistic form during the period when he was writing his own first two novels, *Thomas l'obscur* and *Aminadab*.

In "Literature and the Right to Death" Blanchot traces the relationship of the novel to the world. He does this by subsuming the novel under the vaguer category of the literary work. The shift of flower to woman is not the only hint of his concern with the novel as a paradigm of the literary work. The essay ends with a discussion of Kafka and includes a crucial but fleeting allusion to Flaubert, a writer who receives suspiciously little attention in the early essays of Blanchot.

It is the other side of death that focuses the discussion of the world, not the murdering power of the name, but the subject's death. At the fulcrum of this change of emphasis lies an important trace of Kierkegaard's theory of language. The formula that language speaks in Adam undergoes a quasi-Hegelian transformation: "Therefore it is accurate to say, when I speak: death speaks in me."

In elaborating this dictum, Blanchot uses the concept of death to establish the ground of a peculiar intersubjective understanding. In the act of speaking, death "is there between us as the distance that separates us, but this distance is also what prevents us from being separated, because it contains the condition of any understanding." In the passages which follow Blanchot makes it clear that the act of self-naming which is a prerequisite for all speech constitutes a denial of self-presence, which immediately entails a repudiation of whatever gets said. By implication both members of the couple "we" become parallel fictions.

Death is an essential force in the course of the Understanding in *The Phenomenology of Mind*. His essay is an allegorical reading of parts of the *Phenomenology* in which the tensions between Hegel's epistemological subjects and objects are shifted, apparently, to writers and readers. The understanding Blanchot describes involves the writers and the fictional entity *(l'être que j'interpelle)* who is simultaneously summoned and killed by a linguistic act. The "self-allegory" (Mallarmé's term) of this shadow world of language and literature at this point is Blanchot's own version of a "tombeau" poem, in this case, a prose poem on the impossibility of dying: the "tombeau" of Lazarus. In the transpositional sequence self-naming becomes "mon chant funèbre," the noun objectifies itself as "une pierre tombale pesant sur le vide." The speech act

"*Lazare, veni foras*" restitutes only "l'obscure réalité cadaverique" but it represents, in a Hegelian phrase, "la vie de l'esprit."

What does Blanchot make out of "the life of the spirit"? By jumping from Hegel to Mallarmé and by introducing the figure of Lazarus as the representative of the process he called "dread" in "From Dread to Language," he derives a dialectical presentation of the life of the spirit as the discrepancy between language and existence. That discrepancy characterizes literary language.

Four times in the essay Blanchot repeats the phrase "la vie porte la mort et se maintient dans la mort même," with minimal variation. Typically he does not identify the source of the phrase. One looks in vain for its reference in all the published Blanchot criticism. But presumably that is below the dignity of Blanchot's professional readers. However we cannot avoid the importance of these ignored — and harassingly difficult — quotations.

In this case the phrase "that endures [death] and maintains itself in it" is a translation of "das ihn erträgt und in ihm sich erhält," from the Preface to Hegel's *The Phenomenology of Mind*. To understand Blanchot's fecund misuse of this phrase we should consider its original context, even though it is powerfully suppressed in "Literature and the Right to Death."

At the point in the Preface to which Blanchot's quotation alludes Hegel expounds the power of the *der Verstand* (Miller: "the Understanding") in a lanugage rich with undercurrents of aesthetic and theological polemic. Hegel's paragraph in full reads:

> The *analysis* of an idea, as it used to be carried out, was, in fact, nothing else than ridding it of the form in which it had become familiar. To break an idea up into its original elements is to return to its moments, which at least do not have the form of the given idea, but rather constitute the immediate property of the self. This analysis, to be sure, only arrives at *thoughts* which are themselves familiar, fixed, and inert determinations. But what is thus *separated* and non-actual is an essential moment; for it is only because the concrete does divide itself, and make itself into something non-actual, that it is self-moving. The activity of dissolution is the power and work of the *Understanding*, the most astonishing

and mightiest of powers, or rather the absolute power. The circle that remains self-enclosed and, like substance, holds its moments together, is an immediate relationship, one therefore which has nothing astonishing about it. But that an accident as such, detached from what circumscribes it, what is bound and is actual only in its context with others, should attain an existence of its own and a separate freedom—this is the tremendous power of the negative; it is the energy of thought, of the pure 'I'. Death, if that is what we want to call this non-actuality, is of all things the most dreadful, and to hold fast what is dead requires the greatest strength. Lacking strength, Beauty hates the Understanding for asking of her what it cannot do. But the life of Spirit is not the life that shrinks from death and keeps itself untouched by devastation, but rather the life that endures it and maintains itself in it. It wins its truth only when, in utter dismemberment, it finds itself. It is this power, not as something positive, which closes its eyes to the negative, as when we say of something that it is nothing or is false, and then, having done with it, turn away and pass on to something else; on the contrary, Spirit is this power only by looking the negative in the face, and tarrying with it. This tarrying with the negative is the magical power that converts it into being. This power is identical with what we earlier called the Subject, which by giving determinateness an existence in its own element supersedes abstract immediacy, i.e. the immediacy which barely is, and thus is authentic substance: that being or immediacy whose mediation is not outside of it but which is this mediation itself.[2]

When we focus upon the more immediate context of Blanchot's excision, we find a network of interesting allusions. Of the apparently tangential references, Blanchot might well have been aware. In the footnotes to Hyppolite's translation can be found the identification of "Die kraftlose Schönheit" (translated here, "Lacking strength, Beauty") with the Romantic cult of beauty. The association of the key phrase, "that endures it and maintains itself in it," with the passion and resurrection of Christ is made by Hyppolite near the end of his two volume commentary. Finally, the Dionysiac overtone of "der absoluten Zerris-

---

[2] Wilhelm Hegel, *Phenomenology of Spirit*, Trans. A.V. Miller, (Oxford: Oxford University Press, 1977) pp. 18-19.

senheit" ("utter dismemberment") would not have been lost on an author who dwelled for three decades on the meaning of the myth of Orpheus.

Embedded in Hegel's meditation on the Understanding is a rejection of a version of Jesus that would see him as a "beautiful soul"—a position to which he had been rather sympathetic in his earliest theological writings. In emphasizing the transitive force of Christ's passion, Hegel does not hesitate to associate the crucifixion with Hellenic *sparagmos*.

If indeed literary language is "das Leben des Geistes," then the Gospel allusions take on a new function. Obviously for Blanchot they are not keys to a revelation, to the *logos*. Yet their privileged status arises from their fictional nature and their discursive ambition. The Bible as the locus of the simultaneity of fiction and transcendental truth represents the quintessential case of literature. Many years later in "The Absence of the Book" he will come to an explicit formulation of this, again invoking Hegel and Mallarmé.

Blanchot suggests the New Testament is an allegory of its own quest for transcendental authority. The possibility for the failure of its claims fascinates him. His negative version of the scriptures is populated by the doubting Thomas, Christ who cannot be touched (or read, as in Blanchot's ironic reformulation *Noli me legere*), the unresurrected Lazarus, and even Moses at the moment of his denial by Yahweh, as we shall shortly see.

In Blanchot's version of Hegel, Christ's encounter with death is less His own "life that endures it and maintains itself in it," than His calling forth of Lazarus. In one of the central texts which announce the "modern" sensibility, *The Painter of Modern Life*, Charles Baudelaire used the Lazarus formula to describe the new mode of representation:

> . . . the first is the absorbed intenseness of a resurrecting and evocative memory, a memory that says to every object: "Lazarus, arise"; the second is a fire, an intoxication of pencil or brush, almost amounting to frenzy. This is the fear of not going fast enough, of letting the spectre escape before the synthesis has been extracted and taken possession of, the terrible fear that takes hold of all great artists and fills them with such an ardent desire to appropriate all means of expression, so that the commands of the mind may

never be weakened by the hand's hesitation; so that, in the end, the ideal execution may become as unconscious, as flowing, as the process of digesting is for the brain of a healthy man after dinner.[3]

Baudelaire here unwittingly prophesies the spontaneity of visualization which was to become a cornerstone of modernist poetics. In contrast, Blanchot's unique version of Lazarus locates the thrust of literary language in a resistance to a mode of representation that would be dominantly visual. Baudelaire's modernity would be a form of the encounter "in dem er dem Negativen ins Angesicht schaut" ("which looks the negative in the face").

Thus, the difficulty of facing up to the Negative cannot even be circumvented by gazing upon the divine presence. Blanchot says as much by introducing—as always elliptically—the Moses of Exodus 33:18 who is denied in his desperate request to see God directly. The Vulgate says, *non enim videbit me homo et vivet*. This Blanchot renders, "whoever sees God dies." Like Moses, language, that is, literary language, seeks an unmediated presence which it cannot attain. "Something has disappeared." This is the specificity of existence as that which is both ontologically and temporally prior. In a powerful collapsing of the Lazarus theme upon Mallarmé's olfactory invocation in "Crise de Vers," he restates the quest of literature as the resurrection of "the Lazarus of the tomb and not the Lazarus brought back into the daylight, the one who already smells bad, who is Evil, Lazarus lost not Lazarus saved and brought back to life. *I say a flower!*"

Where Mallarmé's verbal flower arose as "l'absente de tous bouquets," Blanchot invents the putrifying corpse of Lazarus as the material reality of words which contrast strongly with the necessarily evanescent images they evoke. The transposition of Mallarmé's text into Blanchot's sinuous argument is very evident here. Its idealism is barely displaced into the quasi-Hegelian context of the earlier part of the essay. Although the "idée même" does not make an appearance here, it is not far off. For the opposition of "the double condition of the word, crude or immediate here, there essential" (Mallarmé, "Crise de Vers") is the implicit basis of the transition Blanchot makes.

[3] Charles Baudelaire, *Selected Writings on Art and Artists*, trans. P.B. Charvet (London: Penguin, 1972) p. 408.

Blanchot dwells upon the literariness of literature. Curiously, he finds it presented more overtly in the philosophical tradition than in the poetic: Kierkegaard enters the first text to illuminate Mallarmé and Balzac; in the other, Hegel contains the essence of Mallarmé and Ponge. "Death" figuratively determines the temporality of Blanchot's writings. It is an oxymoron which turns the concepts of origin and *telos* into paradoxes. At the conclusion of "Literature and the Right to Death," he glimpses a sightless vision of the origin of literature, which the essay has sought:

> This original double meaning, which lies deep inside every word like a condemnation that is still unknown and a happiness that is still invisible, is the source of literature, because literature is the form this double meaning has chosen in which to show itself behind the meaning and value of words, and the question it asks is the question asked by literature.

The possibility of death which fascinates Blanchot is the impossibility of an end to literature. The ultimate model for the "parole" (speech), as a concealed curse and a stroke of fortune yet to be seen, would be Yahweh's injunction to Adam. Blanchot repeats an irony on which Christian theology has thrived: the happy fall of Adam provoked a greater gift than Edenic immortality. Yet the modernity of Blanchot demonstrates itself in his elliptical omission of the salvation. Death itself figuratively stands for the whole of the divine promise. If we read no further than the fourth chapter of Genesis, we see that that one promise is fulfilled. But even the scene in Genesis, Chapter 2, cannot be identified as the irreducible moment of origin for literature; for the myth of Eden is the narrative elaboration of the earlier moment of the *fiat lux*. And before that literary ventriloquism of the Word of God could appear in Genesis, two verses were required to set the scene. Blanchot points to this infinite regress when he declares that literature is the form origin picked in which to manifest itself.

In "Two Versions of the Imaginary" (1951) Blanchot investigated the nature of literary images in terms which recollect Lévinas' book *Existence and Existents*. Blanchot would never identify the image with the presencing of being, but it curiously resembles Lévinas' *"il y a"* (there is . . .). "When there is nothing," Blanchot writes immediately after posing the question, "What is the image?," "that is where the image finds its condition, but disappears into it. The image requires the neutrality and the effacement of the world . . . " Inevitably this aesthetic wiping out of the world is achieved by death, the peculiarly unfamiliar version of death which Blanchot repeatedly introduces into his theoretical texts.

"At first sight, the image does not resemble a cadaver, but it could be that the strangeness of a cadaver is also the strangeness of the image." The dialectical function of the image, he tells us, is to mediate between "here" and "nowhere." In apposition to the image, stands "la dépouille." Where Lévinas sought out the analogies of Shakespearean ghosts, Blanchot presses the meaning of Hamlet's "mortal coil" (*dépouille mortelle*) until the corpse becomes an allegory of mimesis. Since it is both here and nowhere "the cadaverous presence establishes a relation between here and nowhere." The cadaver is not the person who has "departed" but it comes to resemble him. In fact, through Blanchot's logic it becomes the essence of resemblance. It is important to him that that which it resembles is no longer, is, in fact, nothing. The identification of the immediate past with nothing is consistent with Blanchot's radical treatment of time as that which absolutely escapes literature and which renders it cadaverous. In this temporalization of representation Blanchot comes closest to Baudelaire's *The Painter of Modern Life* (as quoted, pages 178-79) even though he assigns a negative value to the resurrected image where Baudelaire remained enthusiastic about it.

He alludes to Poe's *The Fall of the House of Usher* here (Baudelaire had stressed "The Man in the Crowd" in *The Painter of Modern Life*) and interprets it thus:

> The dear departed, then, is conveyed to another place, and undoubtedly the site is only symbolically at a distance, in no way unlocatable, but it is nevertheless true that the *here* of *here lies*, full of names, of solid constructions, of affirmations of identity, is preeminently the anonymous and impersonal place, as though, within the limits drawn for it and in the vain guise of a pretention capable of surviving everything, the monotony of an infinite ero-

sion were at work obliterating the living truth that characterizes every place, and making it equal to the absolute neutrality of death.

The passivity of the tomb and its inscription of time allows for death to triumph over even the place where it is named. The meteorological destruction suggests to Blanchot, in the subsequent paragraph, the slow murders of obsessive poisoners, who delight in the very temporal extension of their work. "By poisoning time . . . they brush with horror." The implication here is that the poisoner deludes himself into an identification with time itself. Time, as "the horror," in this essay comes close to the dreadful repetition which brings Lévinas in contact with Being.

Nor is the divine absent from Blanchot's consideration. "Man is made in his own image: this is what we learn from the strangeness of the resemblance of cadavers. But this formula should first of all be understood this way: *man is unmade according to his image*. The image . . . has nothing to resemble."

The *his* is deliberately ambiguous in a context where the body resembles itself. But Genesis 1:26 is obviously behind this referential indetermination. "Et ait: Faciamus hominem ad imaginem et similitudinem nostram . . . Et creavit Deus hominem ad imaginem suam: ad imaginem Dei creavit illum, masculum et feminam creavit eos." Blanchot takes Lévinas' version of the sublime into a gnosticism of his own. *Unmake according to* . . . defies sense if not grammar. But the rupture with meaning is what is most at stake in the discussion of the image, as the rest of the paragraph labors to affirm.

The difference between man and his image here repeats the Biblical difference between God and man. In fact, the ambiguous coupling of "image" and "resemblance" is congruent with the tension between *imaginem* and *similitudinem* in the passage from Genesis. The formula "*Lazare, veni foras*," reappears in the essay "Reading" (1952) where it describes the liberating act of reading. But here the words are addressed to the stone itself, not to the corpse. The tombstone, which represents the literary text, responds with a "vast deluge of stone, that shakes the earth and the sky." This hyperbolically reflects the rolling gravestone invoked by Mallarmé in his "Tombeau" sonnet to Verlaine. The difference between writing and reading is inscribed in the variations of Blanchot's figure. Writing summons the corpse and in so doing reinforces the covering stone with the materiality of language; that materiality comes forth to the same beckoning formula of the reader. The resurrected Lazarus, as the transparency of linguistic reference, the adequation of language to existence, and the perfect recovery of past time, has no place in Blanchot's allegory; or rather, occupies as purely negative place, the marker of a frustrated and impossible *telos*.

A foreign reader, or a late reader, who encounters Blanchot's criticism only in the books which he assembled out of his contributions to periodicals, must be struck by the difference between *L'Espace littéraire* and its predecessor, *La Part du feu*. Not only did the portion of theoretical articles come to outnumber the critical texts, but the very issues shifted. The concern with death remained, of course. Yet the status of the writer no longer preoccupied Blanchot's mind. Now the interplay of two concepts "work" and "book" mould his argument. The meditation on "work" is a refinement of his earlier concern with *the author* and his "dread." Just as Kierkegaard guided the thought in "From Dread to Language" and Hegel that of "Literature and the Right to Death," even when those essays move in deliberately anti-Kierkegaardian and anti-Hegelian directions, the aesthetics of Heidegger resound throughout *L'Espace littéraire*. In 1950 his collection of essays, *Holzwege*, appeared, making available in German the crucial study of 1935-6, "The Origin of the Work of Art." Heidegger's examination of the concept of *Werk* in works of art may have engaged Blanchot in his meditations on *l'oeuvre*. In Albert Hofstadter's translation of Heidegger we find:

> Yet is the work ever in itself accessible? To gain access to the work, it would be necessary to remove it from all relations to something other than itself, in order to let it stand on its own for itself alone. But the artist's most peculiar intention already aims in this direction. The work is to be released by him to its pure self-subsistence . . .
> Where does a work belong? The work belongs, as work, uniquely

within the realm that is opened up by itself. For the work-being of
the work is present in, and only in, such opening up. We said that
in the work there was a happening of truth at work.[4]

Blanchot puts Heidegger under a negative sign. While he allows the
centrality of the concept of "work" to thinking about art, he insists that a
move from work to truth, or any other valorization of work misses the
essential dialectic of work; for him, the masterpiece is not the product of
the "passageway" from "work," as Heidegger claims, but the regrettable
sign of the work's disappearance.

In L'Espace littéraire the tomb scenes from the Gospel of John provide a frame around a retelling of the myth of Orpheus. For the preface
to the collection the author wrote a single paragraph, which I shall
translate in its entirety:

> A book, even a fragmentary one, has a center which attracts it;
> not a fixed center, but one which shifts under pressure from the
> book and the circumstances of its composition. A fixed center too,
> which shifts, if it is genuine, by staying the same and always becom-
> ing more central, more hidden, more wavering and more pressing.
> The writer of the book writes it out of desire, out of ignorance of this
> center. The feeling of having touched it might only be the illusion
> of having hit it; when it is a matter of a book of illuminations, there
> is something of a methodical fairness in telling toward what point
> the book seems to steer: here, towards the pages called "The Gaze
> of Orpheus."

As Blanchot recounts it the story of Orpheus is another version of the
labor of the Negative which we enocuntered in the Preface to *The
Phenomenology of Mind.* In Lydia Davis's translation we read:
"Eurydice lost and Orpheus scattered are necessary to the song, just as
the ordeal of eternal worklessness is necessary to the work." Blanchot
recognizes the story of Orpheus as an allegory of the Life of the Mind,
which Hegel tells us "wins its truth only in utter dismemberment when
it finds itself." Both the lost Eurydice and the scattered Orpheus are
figures of "die absolute Zerrissenheit."

[4] Martin Heidegger, *Poetry, Language, Thought,* trans. A. Hofstadter (New York:
Harper and Row, 1975) pp. 40-41.

Another name for the persistence of the work of Negation in Blanchot's text is "the other night." If we look back in the collection L'Espace littéraire to the essay which precedes "The Gaze of Orpheus" we see that "the other night" is a formula for the dialectic of appearance and disappearance. In "Le Dehors, la nuit" Blanchot writes: "But when everything has disappeared into the night, 'everything has disappeared' appears. This is the *other* night. The night is the apparition of 'everything has disappeared.' It is what is intimated when dreams replace sleep, when the dead go into the depths of the night, when the depths of the night appears in those who have disappeared."

The movement from "the night" to "the other night" is Hegelian, but the penumbra of ghosts around that enigmatic light is Blanchot's own obsessive interpretation of Hegel's naked "Tod." It is another Blanchotian peculiarity, and a particularly intriguing one, to identify the movement of this dialectic with "inspiration."

But an even more surprising extension of the mythopoeic use of Orpheus occurs in "The Power and the Glory," which Blanchot wrote five years later and placed at the conclusion of Le Livre à venir. There he identifies Eurydice with the illusion of a reading public. This is his most definitive analysis of the politics of writing and reading. Here he insists that the writer must betray his insights into the aporias of reading if he is to be duped into imagining a "reading public."

At the beginning of Le Livre à venir he allegorized the Homeric episode of the Sirens as the paradigm for the récit (which has been translated "tale" throughout). After his initial description of Ulysses' encounter with the Sirens in terms that evoke at one point the master-slave dialectic of The Phenomenology of Mind (the crew of Ulysses experiences "the satisfaction of gaining mastery over their master") Blanchot asserts in the first line of the section "The secret law of the tale": "This is not an allegory. A very obscure struggle takes place between every tale and the encounter with the Sirens, that enigmatic song which is powerful because of its failure."

Blanchot's use of the myth of the Sirens is not an allegory, simply because he conservatively insists on a restricted high Romantic definition of allegory, which excludes the viability of any modern allegory. Nevertheless, "The Song of the Sirens," like "The Gaze of Orpheus," which formed the acknowledged center piece of his previous collection *L'Espace littéraire*, is an outstanding example of the allegorizing tendency of Blanchot's criticism during the 1950's. He freely develops a myth of literature in a lacuna of the ancient text he names as his source. Where the *Odyssey* has nothing to say about the specifics of the Sirens' devastating song, Blanchot invents, not a content, but an enigma which corresponds to the tensions between literature and its lacks in his earlier essays. Even the *Odyssey* itself as the source text for the myth of the Sirens plays the role of the gravestone: "They enticed him to a place which he did not want to fall into and, hidden in the heart of the *Odyssey*, which had become their tomb, they drew him — and many others — into that happy, unhappy voyage which is the voyage of the tale of a song which is no longer immediate, but is narrated, and because of this made to seem harmless, an ode which has turned into an episode."

In "Literature and the Right to Death" Blanchot referred to Stoicism, Skepticism, and the Unhappy Consciousness as phases of the writer's relationship to his work. This observation is more subtly embedded in "The Song of the Sirens" in the dialectical description of Ulysses' "victory" over the Sirens. Here Blanchot calls Ulysses a figure of decadence, unworthy to be the hero of the *Iliad*, because he wins without risk or consequences. Thus he establishes, albeit fragmentarily, a history of epic and novel parallel to that of Lukács in *The Theory of the Novel*. For Blanchot the epic, and later the lyric ("ode"), have no intrinsic importance: they occupy the negative pole in distinction to which the novel and the *récit* can be sketched. The illusionary mastery of the crew is incorporated into this context. They do not hear the "ode" of the Sirens but witness the silly contortions of their captain; their satisfaction corresponds to what Hegel calls Stoicism. But Ulysses himself enters into a more complex relationship with the Sirens:

> Ulysses' attitude, the amazing deafness of a man who is deaf because he can hear, was enough to fill the Sirens with a despair which until then had been felt only by men, and this despair turned them into real and beautiful girls, just this once real and worthy of their promise, and therefore capable of vanishing into the truth and depth of their song.

The crew could neither hear nor understand, but they could see; and of what they saw, they conceived a new interpretation of the power relationship between themselves and the captain who ordered and limited their movement. Ulysses could hear and understand, but he could not act, that is, respond with anything but understanding. The error of pure visibility underlies the allegory at this point. Elsewhere Blanchot reads the Unhappy Consciousness as an allegory for this evasion. In the reciprocal dialectic the Sirens themselves become figures of this same Unhappy Consciousness which teases them into a semi-humanity. This reflexive movement itself reflects the earlier logic by which Ulysses comes to understand that the seductive inhumanity of the Sirens' song reveals that the seductiveness of all human song is a measure of its inhumanity. Thus the Sirens as representatives of the imaginary world are simply figures of a specular movement which is never totally efficient and which derives its power from the measure of its insufficiency. As a system *The Phenomenology of Mind* should constitute a totally efficient reflexive machine. The dialectic of literature finds itself at the stage of the Unhappy Consciousness; Hegel's dialectical leap into reason looks to Blanchot like a cover-up for the fecund mess which has been revealed at the borders of self-consciousness. Blanchot's approach to the critical discussion of this revelation is to reinterpret older texts—Hegel's, Homer's—as allegories of their own self-insufficiency. For the moment, the undefined ideal of epic or "ode" contains the possibility of transcribing the Sirens' song or reenacting the authenticity of its encounter. However, narrative fiction substitutes a description of the setting, the force-field, of the encounter. The mediating element, which defuses the destructive "song" by recounting it, is nothing more than the narrator's use of time, but Blanchot suspends this conclusion until the second part of his essay, "L'Experience de Proust,"[5] which he originally published in the number of the N.R.F. following the one in which "The Song of the Sirens" first appeared.

Blanchot has more in mind in this essay than a restatement of "Literature and the Right to Death"; this is the place where he will distinguish

[5] This essay will appear in a volume of Blanchot's essays edited by Gabriel Josipovici and Sacha Rabinovitch (who is also the translator), to be published by Harvester Press (Brighton, England).

the *roman* (novel) from the *récit* (tale), a discrimination valuable to all readers of his fiction, which divides itself into those two categories. However, it will not be easy for a reader to apply this distinction to literary works. Nerval's *Aurélia*, Rimbaud's *Une Saison en enfer*, and Breton's *Nadja* are the three clear-cut cases for the *récit* which he offers. However, *Moby Dick* and *A La Recherche du temps perdu* are also used on the side of the *récit*. For the novel itself, no examples are mentioned. As Blanchot describes them, the *roman* and the *récit* are both born of the encounter of Ulysses and the Sirens. "What lies in the foreground of the novel is the previous voyage, the voyage which takes Ulysses to the moment of the encounter."

Within the limits of this metaphor of sailing, the novel is described as an elaboration of the details and perspectives of the voyage. According to the superstition of the sailors, all reference to the destination must be suppressed. "The rule is therefore silence, discretion, forgetfulness." What must be forgotten is the fascinating insufficiency of the "ode"; its postponement is the genesis of the "episode." Here Blanchot hints at one of his favorite polarities as a definition of narrative movement: "L'attente . . . l'oubli."

The novel "in its discretion and its cheerful nothingness takes upon itself the task of forgetting what others degrade by calling it the essential. Diversion is its profound song." It maintains its fictional status by not swerving from what is credible and familiar. The historical schema reappears here obscurely when Blanchot states that technology has transformed the means of diversion, which, he implies, has severely limited the viability of the novel. This is the point at which he elaborates his theory of the *récit*.

Like the novel it is a movement toward an unknown point. But unlike it it does not elaborate itself in diversion, in the textured network of interlocked digressions. That which the *récit* approaches is the *récit* itself, according to Blanchot. It is then, in Mallarmé's terms, an allegory of itself. "The tale is not the narration of an event, but that event itself, the approach to that event, the place where that event is made to happen—an event which is yet to come and through whose power of attraction the tale can hope to come into being too."

The problematic relationship of literary language to human time permits and encourages this paradoxical genre. Insofar as the *récit* pretends to relate an experience which its narrator has survived to recount, it coincides with the claims and methods of autobiography. The narrator of a *récit*, however, is not the product of biological generation. He is engendered by the needs of the tale itself. As he veers away from the visual clarity of the novel, he brings the reader into contact with ostensible "time."

The flexibility of temporal designations in language permits this anomaly to occur. It in turn engenders the perpetual biographical speculation about the relationship of Nerval to the narrator of *Aurélia*, of Melville to Ahab (Blanchot does not mention Ishmael), Proust to Marcel, of the mysterious and self-effacing Blanchot to the narrator of his *récits*. The literary biographer in this case becomes a single-minded narrator himself.

Blanchot returns to the Vulgate to create a model for the paradox of authorship and authority here: "This seems obscure, it is like the embarrassment the first man would have felt if, in order to be created, he himself had had to pronounce in a completely human way the divine *fiat lux* that would cause his eyes to open." The decadence of narrative fiction is its daring to mimic the role of a divine creator in purely human language. According to Blanchot's interpretation of the myth of the Sirens, this is the possibility Ulysses derives from the Sirens' song. In one of Blanchot's hyperbolic formulae: this recognition turns Ulysses into Homer.

In collapsing the creation of man upon the separation of light from darkness, Blanchot equates all making with the fashioning of a semblance or image. The polarity he develops between Ulysses and Melville's Ahab turns upon the status of the imaginary. "We cannot deny that Ulysses understood something of what Ahab saw, but he stood fast within that understanding, while Ahab became lost in the image." The secularized *fiat lux* stands for all verbal creation. The two versions of that seductive metamorphosis, as Blanchot sets it up, are symbolized by Ulysses who maintains a distance from what draws him and Ahab who engages it to his destruction. In the first case, the imaginary beings are drawn toward the actual world. Ulysses' ruse makes them into "real and beautiful girls." Ahab gives himself over to "that worldless space."

Blanchot can combine these apparently contradictory movements within a single model for the *récit* because spatiality and the status of the image are only secondary concerns for him in this essay; they are in fact visual foils for his articulation of temporality as the basis of both the novel and the *récit* and their discrimination. In the final section of the essay, "The Metamorphosis," he writes:

> . . . what makes the novel move forward is everyday, collective or personal time, or more precisely the desire to urge time to speak; the tale moves forward through that *other* time, it makes that other voyage, which is the passage from the real song to the imaginary song, the movement which causes the real song to become imaginary little by little, though all at once (and this "little by little, though all at once" is the very time of the metamorphosis), to become an enigmatic song always at a distance, designating this distance as a space to be crossed and designating the place to which it leads as the point where singing will cease to be a lure.

In the *récit* the image appears in its temporal form as experience. Its ambiguity derives from the curiosity of a fictional past which literary language renders present, and which in that present moment is concentrated upon what is to come. Blanchot makes no mention of Ishmael in *Moby Dick*, as I have already noted. He writes as if Ahab were the narrator of the story. Nevertheless Melville's use of quotations prefigures Blanchot's; he specifies Ishmael's narrative function by prefacing the epilogue with a repeated phrase from the first chapter of the Book of Job: "And I only am escaped alone to tell thee." The exactitude of the narration is a Satanic torture. "Only . . . alone" the storyteller appears before Job to obliterate his listener's opulent past. By introducing the epilogue of *Moby Dick* with this quotation, Melville not only emphasizes the unique survival of Ishmael, his narrator, but darkly hints that his story is but the overture to more severe trials. This is the very aspect of Melville's book that Blanchot presses without elaborating upon it. The narrator of the *récit* always says, "And I only am escaped alone to tell thee." He acts as if the burden of experience compelled him to recount it. Yet Blanchot recognizes that the compulsion to write engenders the experience just as within the tale the experience engenders the obsessive retelling.

"The Problem of Wittgenstein," "The Narrative Voice," and "The Absence of the Book" appeared in the final section of Blanchot's longest volume, *L'Entretien infini* (1969). The first two had been printed in the *Nouvelle Revue Française* in 1963 and 1964 respectively; the third, which ends Blanchot's volume as well as our collection, was his first contribution to *L'Ephémère*, the journal of the poet Yves Bonnefoy, in 1969. These three essays represented Blanchot's theoretical work in its most developed phase.

Throughout *L'Entretien infini* Blanchot reformulated and elaborated upon the central issues of his critical thinking. For instance, the third essay in that collection, "Parler, ce n'est pas voir," is a dialogue about the resistance to visibility inherent in literary language. When one voice insists that we are not led astray by speech, the other concludes:

> —Perhaps unfortunately: as if we were turned away from the visible without being oriented toward the invisible. I don't know if what I am saying says something. Yet it is simple. To speak is not to see. Speech frees thought from this optical requirement which has dominated our approach to things for thousands of years in the western tradition, and invited us to think under the guarantee of light or under the threat of the absence of light. I'll let you catalogue the words in which there are suggestions that saying the truth has to be thinking according to the standard of the eyes.
>
> —You don't want to oppose one meaning to the other, understanding to sight, do you?
>
> —I wouldn't want to fall into that trap.

This sinuous dialogue, which Blanchot originally entitled "Walking like a crayfish," eventually enters upon the status of the image. Then we find the following argument:

> — . . . Of the image too it is hard to speak rigorously. The image is the duplicity of revelation. What hides while revealing, the veil which reveals while it is covering up again in the ambiguous indecisions of the word "reveal," that's the image. The image is image

in this duplicity, not the double of the object, but the initial doubling which then allows the thing to become a figure; still higher than
the doubling, it is the folding, the turn of the turning, this "version" always about to invert itself, and however in it the here and
there of a divergence. The speech of which we are trying to speak is
the return to this first turning—a noun we have to understand as a
verb, the movement of turning, the dizziness where the vortex, the
leap, and the fall repose. Note that the terms for the directions of
our literary language receive this notion of turning to which, as is
right, poetry makes the clearest allusion in the word "verse," while
"prose" proceeds straight along its road through a detour which
ceaselessly corrects itself.

The nature of imagery and visualization has been an obsession of
poetics and of philosophy since the beginning of Romanticism. The
speculations of Blake, Coleridge, and Wordsworth were reformulated
obliquely in the poetics of Pound, Crane, and Eliot. In more recent
years, the meditations of Sartre, Wittgenstein, and Ryle have enlivened
the debate. Blanchot never confronted the theoreticians of imagery and
imagination directly. The nuances of difference between optical and
noetic vision seem not to interest him. In his criticism, he writes as if the
investigation of imagery, in all of its diversity, were an evasion of something more fundamental to literature: a concept of temporality which
resists all spatial models. His involuted and elegant language is a struggle
to "endure it and maintain itself in it."

The writing of *L'Entretien infini* can often exasperate the Anglo-
American reader with its obscurities and seemingly manneristic
nuances. We must remember that it is the very inadequacy of theoretical language which impels and prolongs Blanchot's prose. The vocabulary of fiction and the vocabulary of the theory of fiction are essentially
the same. It is a language founded upon the value and truth of visibility,
which has to perform contortions to create a space in which visibility can
be examined and in which its unnamed alternatives and opposites can
be propounded. At one point Blanchot identifies this paradox for literary
theory with "the problem of Wittgenstein," the lack of a metalanguage
in which the pitfalls of ordinary language within philosophical dis-
courses might logically be examined. Yet Blanchot sees this not only as a

dilemma for philosophical literary criticism, but for self-conscious novelists such as Flaubert and Roussel.

In 1963, in an essay on René Char, Blanchot developed an analogy from the history of Greek prose into a theoretical tool which he employed frequently in the 1960s. He had read that Heraclitus created abstract terms by making neuter nouns out of verbal adjectives and adverbs. He wrote:

> The unknown is verbally a neuter. The discretion of the French language, which does not use a neuter gender, is inconvenient, but finally not without merit, for what the neuter has is not a third gender in opposition to the two others which constitutes a fixed class of existing or logical beings. The neuter is something which occurs in every gender: the non-general, the non-generic, like the non-particular. It rejects determination in the category of the object as well as the subject.

Robert Lamberton suggested that Blanchot's term "Le neutre" should be rendered "the neutral" in English. There is considerable merit and insight in this suggestion. Nevertheless the grammatical term "neuter" has been retained to preserve the irritability of the French text.

"Le neutre" implies a neutrality toward the visibility and invisibility of language. The very absence of a neuter case in French gives to the common pronoun "il" the ambiguous designation of both "he" and "it." Blanchot directed his attention to this ambiguity and its implications in the essay "The Narrative Voice," which he subtitled "le 'il', le neutre."

Apparently Blanchot had not read Kafka until after he wrote his second novel, *Aminadab* (1942). Sartre noted the similarity of that novel to Kafka's major works in his early essay on Blanchot (translated by Annette Michelson in Sartre's *Literary and Philosophical Essays*). Soon after that Kafka became a central figure in Blanchot's critical work. Three essays in *La Part du feu* were devoted to him. In one of them, "Kafka et la littérature," which had first appeared in the *Cahiers de la Pléiade*, in 1949, he seized upon Kafka's definition of literary language as the "passage du *Ich* au *Er*, du *Je* au *Il*." This transformation of *I* to *He* reechoes throughout Blanchot's theoretical work and dominates important passages in *L'Espace littéraire*. Fifteen years later, in "The Narrative Voice," Blanchot maintains that it is not the objectivity of this transformation, but its neutrality that characterizes the narrative voice.

Of course, Blanchot does not mean that there is a semantic ambiguity when we read the word "il" in a French novel. Rather he asserts that the writing of fiction, in all of its forms, entails the marshalling of "unknown" linguistic possibilities, just as the use of the neuter singular noun in the Greek of Heraclitus opened a realm of unknown entities to philosophical thinking.

From the beginning of his critical endeavor Blanchot stressed, in writing, the aporias of writing. Philosophical and literary texts, according to his reading of them, gesture in directions beyond the confines of syntax and lexicography. "Dread," "death," "the neuter," and "worklessness," are terms he has employed to designate the different relationships the writer and the written text have toward what they cannot explicitly say.

Blanchot does not tire of reformulating his central insights. "The Absence of the Book" both repeats and diverges from "Literature and the Right to Death," which he published more than twenty years earlier. The same constellations of fixed points—Hegel, Mallarmé, the Bible—describe and elaborate the tensions between any book, however ambitious and "complete," and the anonymous energy of "The Work" which initiates and sustains the writer's vocation. The importance of the Bible in Blanchot's concept of the authoritative book is much more explicit in this later essay than it had been in the earlier one, where it hovered on the penumbra of allusion and quotations that were slightly askew. This directness in no way simplifies his thought; for out of his meditations on the Bible there emerges a dialectical expression of authority which he calls "the Law," a problematic coordinate of writing which has haunted Blanchot's other writing, his fiction, from the beginning.

To explicate Blanchot's concept of "law," then, we would have to turn from "The Absence of the Book" to a series of books he called his "romans" and "récits." One step in that direction for the American reader would be to read Lydia Davis's translation of "*The Madness of the Day*" (Station Hill, bilingual edition, 1981); another, more problematical, step might be to read Jacques Derrida's baroque commentary on that *récit*, which appeared in *Glyph* 7 (Johns Hopkins, 1980) conveniently in both English and French.

Reading Blanchot involves us in a maze of detours and repetitions. The exasperations and bewilderments of this unguided tour are numerous and persistent. The reward is an engagement with a uniquely tenacious mind that had relentlessly stuck to, dwelled upon, the most difficult problems that literature poses. Writing of "the clarity" of Blanchot's critical writings, Paul de Man observed: "Nothing, in fact, could be more obscure than the nature of this light." Blanchot propounds no doctrine, but by making "literature" less visible, more deadly, he challenges and thrills us with a theory of reading and writing as a solitary defense against the delusions of prefabricated clarity.